FACETS OF LIBRARY AND INFORMATION SCIENCE

FACETS OF LIBRARY AND INFORMATION SCIENCE

By

PROF. A. A. N. RAJU

Formerly Head, Dept. of Library & Information Science

Osmania University,

HYDERABAD - 500 007

Ess Ess Publications

New Delhi

Facets of Library and Information Science

ISBN: 978-81-7000-674-9

Rs.750/-

First Published 2012

Published by:
Ess Ess Publications
4831/24, Ansari Road,
Darya Ganj,
New Delhi-110 002.
INDIA
Phones: 23260807, 41563444
Fax: 41563334
E-mail: info@essessreference.com
www.essessreference.com

Cover Design by *Patch Creative Unit*

Printed and bound in India at Salasar Imaging Systems.

Dedicated To

PROF. N. LAXMAN RAO

My colleague who stood by me through thick and thin of
my two decades of Headship of the
Dept. of Library & Information Science
Osmania University
Hyderabad

CONTENTS

PREFACE

The present volume ***Facets of Library and Information Science*** is a collection of essays written by me during my professional career spanning three and half decades at the Dept. of Library and Information Science, Osmania University, Hyderabad. Some of these essays were published in professional journals and some other were presented at National, Regional and State level Seminars, Conferences and Workshops.

The twenty two essays presented in this Volume are divided into six broad facets viz. ***1. Public Libraries, 2. Library Classification, 3. LIS Curriculum, 4. LIS Research, 5. Legal Deposit*** and ***6.Other Facets.***

The Essays under ***Facet 1. Public Libraries,*** deals with Conversation and Preservation of Documents in Public Libraries and the National Knowledge Commission's Recommendations on Public Library Services.

The four Essays, under ***Facet 2. Library Classification*** deals with international perspective of library classification, features and the developments in UDC IME.1993, and treatment of Fine Arts and Indology in UDC and CC.

The Essays under ***Facet 3. LIS Curriculum,*** deal with the developments in LIS Curriculum and Marketing and Information Technology (IT) Component in the syllabi of MLISc Courses offered by Indian Library Schools.

Facet 4. LIS Research includes essays dealing with importance of historical research in LIS, trends and developments, publication and research activity in the Departments of LIS, Prerequisites for LIS teaching and research in Telugu at the University level, and need for user education programmes to research scholars in Social Sciences.

Fact 5. Legal Deposit consists of three essays on the working of Press and Registration of Books Act, 1867, the Delivery of Books and News Papers (Public Libraries) Act, 1954 and the Indian Copyright Act, 1957 and the role of these three Acts in achieving bibliographical control over Indian Publications.

The five essays included under ***Facet 6. Other Aspects,*** deal with Bibliographic organization and control in Social Sciences, the State of our documentary heritage, Glossaries of LIS terms in Telugu, an Analysis of festschrift volumes brought out in honor of LIS professionals, Need for good library support services to distance learners and Teaching of Reference Service for B.Lib.Sc. Students.

These essays were written during the past four decades and reflect the trends and developments of that period in the subject fields listed under six broad facets. Therefore, one cannot expect latest developments in the twenty two essays. It is sincerely hoped that this volume shall be of immense help to the students, research scholars, faculty members of LIS Departments and practicing librarians who are interested to know the trends and developments in the subject fields of the past decades and presented in these twenty two essays.

Ugadi
Hyderabad

PROF. A. A. N. RAJU

ACKNOWLEDGEMENTS

These essays were published in ILA Bulletin, IASLIC Bulletin, University News and pre-Conference Volumes of ILA, IASLIC and IATL1S National Seminars / Conferences and some of the Festschrift Volumes. I am thankful to them for according permission to publish in the book form.

Sri. Sumit Sethi, the young and dynamic Chief Executive, M/s Ess Ess Publications New Delhi whole heartediy came forward to publish the collection of essays in the form of a book.

Lastly but not the least I would like to thank Sri M. Madhusudan, who prepared preliminary pages and Index of this book.

— PROF. A. A. N. RAJU

Facet 1
PUBLIC LIBRARIES

1
The State of Conservation and Preservation of Documents in Public Libraries

DOCUMENTARY SOURCES

Since time immemorial human beings were communicating with one another through gestures, symbols, sounds, words and written and printed books and other types of documents and of late through electronic media. These documentary sources enabled human civilizations to communicate with each other and thus enrich themselves with the help of this communication process. During the past two thousand years of human civilizations, and even before, it was evident that the intellectual products of human thought and endeavor were being procured, processed, and the thought content embodied in them is disseminated through various methods, and the documents are conserved and preserved in various types of libraries through out the world for posterity.

The World's great libraries viz. National, Public, Academic, Special and Institutional are examples of repositories of human civilization and culture

INDIA'S RICH DOCUMENTARY HERITAGE

India, the cradle of highly developed civilization and culture is dotted with variety of libraries in various parts of the country The growth and development of these libraries accelerated during the lost two centuries. During the Mogul and the British rule a number of Public, Academic and Institutional libraries have been established at important centers of learning in the country. These libraries possess rich, varied, very rare and valuable collections reflecting the political, social, economic and cultural aspects of the country and its people. In essence the documentary sources available in some of the famous, old and prominent public libraries represent and reflect India's cultural heritage in particular and world's heritage in general.

This rich and glorious documentary heritage needs to be properly surveyed, preserved and conserved to the present and future generations as well.

CONSERVATION AND PRESERVATION OF DOCUMENTS

According to the UNESCO's definition *'conservation'* includes those actions involving minimal technical intervention required to prevent further, deterioration to original materials. Such actions are necessary because it is recognized that the original medium, format and content are important for research or other purposes e.g. to retain aesthetic, material, cultural and historical qualities.

'Preservation' on the other hand encompasses all actions required to make documentary heritage accessible for as lone as it is required. It involves controlling the environment and conditions of use and may be included treatment in order to maintain an object, as nearly as possible, in an unchanging state, In case of archival material, moving image and sound, this may

involve transfer to another medium.

A good Preservation Policy must ensure access to information and minimize document deterioration. Thus, preservation and also conservation is the core responsibility of Public Library Services possessing documents of local, regional, national and international importance.

PRESERVATION CONSIDERATIONS

The environment for document collections consists of physical or natural environment and physical conditions. The natural environment to which document collection is exposed has profound effect on their long-term survival.. Aspects of natural environment include: floods, fires, earthquakes and cyclones. These cannot be prevented but strategies can be developed to mitigate their effects.

Specific environmental factors that are harmful to document collections include: heat, humidity, light, air pollution, animals and insects (silver fish, bookworm, termites, moths, cockroaches, rats and mice), poor handling, display practices, and finally vandalism and theft.

The physical conditions included: leaking roofs, broken windows and unstable foundations.

PRESERVATION TECHNIQUES OR PROCEDURES

Some of the important preservation techniques or procedures for books and related material include: binding of books/journals (serials), news papers, repairs to bindings and simple repairs to torn or damaged pages.

Some of the reformatting techniques include — microfilming of newspapers, brittle or fragile paper based materials, copying photographs, copying audiotapes and video materials and electronic digitizing.

Preservation and conservation facilities and equipment include: Conservation laboratory, Paper lamination equipment, bindery, fumigation chamber, microfilming and digitization facility.

Preventive preservation techniques or procedures include: Floor cleaning, shelf cleaning, collection condition surveys, pest inspections, environmental monitoring and a plan for disaster preparedness and response plan.

PUBLIC LIBRARY SCENARIO IN THE COUNTRY

Public libraries have been established during the British rule in various parts of the country by individual and institutional initiatives and support. The growth and development of these libraries has been accelerated after independence. Many state governments in the country have enacted public library laws. The result of this library legislation was orderly development of Public Libraries. These include: State Central Libraries (SCLs), Regional Libraries (RLs), District Central Libraries (DCLs) and Branch Libraries (BLs). Beside these prominent institutions and societies have established and maintaining the public libraries. Some of these libraries are two centuries old. These are called Private or Aided Libraries.

Some of these libraries established during the 19th and beginning of the 20th century possess rich, varied, rare and invaluable documentary sources, which require immediate attention and action for preservation and conservation.

NATURE OF DOCUMENTARY COLLECTIONS

The documentary collections available in some of the old and famous public libraries both government and private include: paper and palm leaf MSS. Especially the collections available in some of the prominent public libraries in South India are in Sanskrit, Tamil, Telugu, Kannada, Malayalam, Arabic, Persian, Urdu, Marathi and of course in English. A variety of subjects in the fields of Sciences, Arts, Humanities and Science and Technology is covered by the MSS, printed books and other types of documents. The rich and varied collections deal with branches of Philosophy, Religion, Culture, Fine Arts, Architecture, Medicine, Agriculture,

Literature, Linguistics, Music, Astrology, Archaeology, Astronomy and Technology.

URGENT NEED

The valuable documentary collections in the prominent and old public libraries in various parts of the country mirror the culture and civilization of India and the richness of Indian languages and also social, political and cultural conditions of the people. These libraries regarded as social and cultural institutions of the nation and reflect the documentary heritage of our country.

There is an urgent need to conserve and preserve such invaluable documentary collections. Laxity on the part of the Central / State Governments may cause immense damage to these rich documentary collections. The protection and safeguards extended to our ancient sites, monuments and buildings through legislative and administrative measures should equally be extended to our rare and invaluable library collections available in the public and other libraries.

UNESCO'S INITIATIVE

Unesco in the year 1992 launched 'Memory of the World Programme' to protect and promote world documentary heritage. The objectives of this programme are four fold. 1. to facilitate preservation by appropriate techniques, 2. to assist access to documentary heritage, 3. to increase awareness worldwide and 4. to promote programme and its products to the widest possible public. Under this programme, UNESCO in collaboration with IFLA has brought out three valuable documents viz:

1. *Memory of the World : General Guidelines to safeguard Documentary Heritage,* 1995.
2. *Memory of the World : A Survey of Current Library Preservation Activities,* 1996, and
3. *Memory of the World: Lost Memory - Libraries and Archives destroyed in 20th Century,* 1996.

It has also brought out another valuable publication titled *Safeguarding our Documentary Heritage*, published in 2000. These four documents provide very valuable and authentic information on our World Documentary Heritage, its present status and guidelines for preservation and conservation.

RRRLF'S ROLE

RRRLF has come in to being in 1972 for the cause of Public Library Development in the country. Through its various programmes, it is assisting the public libraries in various states for collection development, building construction, manpower training and organizing seminars and conferences. In its training programmes it must also assist the concerned authority for organizing short-term and long-term programmes in conservation and preservation of documentary collections. It also must support the infrastructure facilities for preservation and conservation of rare and valuable documents in public libraries. In collaboration with the National and State Archives Departments, the required manpower in conservation and preservation can be trained through short-term and long-term programmes. It can also assist each State Government by providing mobile laboratory for treatment of old and fragile documents available in some old public libraries with necessary equipment and expertise.

WHAT LIES AHEAD

The authorities at the state and national levels should give due thought and attention to the state of affairs of conservation and preservation of documents in our prominent public libraries and initiate suitable actions to safeguard documentary collections, which are at present in pathetic condition in some of the old and prominent public libraries. The managements of some of the old and prominent public libraries were not able to initiate proper action in this regard for want of proper support from the government and other funding agencies. If this pathetic situation continues for long, the present and future generations may lose for ever our rich documentary collections.

The Department of Culture, Ministry of Human Resources Development, Govt. of India may float a national fund as was done in the case of World Heritage Sites' to assist the managements of Public Libraries to preserve and conserve their documentary collections. The state Governments also must lend a helping hand in this regard. Non-Governmental Organisations, Trusts and Industrial Houses and Corporations can also come forward to assist in this endeavor. UNESCO under its 'Memory of the World Programme' may assist some of the old and prominent public libraries to conserve and preserve their rich and valuable documentary collections. This problem is very acute and burning in such public libraries which have been established during the 19th and the beginning of the 20th centuries.

REFERENCES

1. *Memory of the World: General Guidelines to safeguard Documentary Heritage.* Paris, UNESCO, 1995.
2. Raju, A. A. N : 2003 *Documentary Heritage of Indian Libraries.* New Delhi, Ess Ess Publications.
3. ...., 2002 Whether our Documentary Heritage *University News.* V 40, N 8, May 6-12 pp. 9-10.
4. ...., 2001 Bhavanalapai gala sradha Grandhlapatla leydemi. *Vaartha* (Telugu Daily) Wednesday, December 12, p.4.

2

National Knowledge Commission (NKC) and Public Library Services

INTRODUCTION

The Government of India constituted the National Knowledge Commission (NKC) in the year 2005 as a "high level advisory body to the Prime Minister of India with a mandate to guide policy and generate reforms". The Prime Minister in his inaugural address to the Commission on 2nd August 2005 stated that "the time has come to create a second wave institution building and of excellence in the fields of education, research and capability building so that we are better prepared for the 21st Century". The Prime Minister further pointed to the role of Public Libraries which can play "an extremely important element of the foundation of a knowledge economy".

CONSTITUTION OF WORKING GROUP ON LIBRARIES

The Commission as one of its first initiatives undertook to review the library services and to examine the present standards of public, private, institutional and specialized libraries and other information centers. A Working Group (WG) on libraries consisting eminent librarians and LIS teachers was constituted "to initiate objective review of current services and standards and to recommend the changes India needs". There were nine terms of reference for the WG on libraries but there is no specific reference to public libraries. To carry out its work, the WG has set up four committees' viz.,

1. Committee and Database Creation and Networking,
2. Committee on Private Collections,
3. Committee to set standards and modalities for collection development and
4. Committee on staffing pattern and staff requirement of libraries.

The WG has made a total of twenty nine recommendations covering areas such as: *LIS Policy, Finance, Library Management, Access and Networking, Private Collections, Digitization and Open Access, Staffing Pattern and Private Public Partnership.*

REFERENCE TO PUBLIC LIBRARIES

There is no specific reference to focus or on Public Libraries in the twenty nine recommendations of the WG. These are general in nature encompassing Public, Academic, Special and on Private collections. But in the appendices to these recommendations, specific recommendations were made on Public libraries with respect to:

1. Collection Development,
2. Kinds of services,
3. Access to collections,
4. Staffing Pattern and Staff requirements.

COLLECTION DEVELOPMENT

With respect to public library collections, the WG in appendix 5 listed the following four broad guidelines.

1. The size and nature of the collection should reflect the population and local requirements.

2. Locally relevant language material should be available.
3. Book purchase should be a continuous process and at least 10% of the book collection should be less than five years old.
4. At least 60% of the library's budget is spent on collection development.

Comment

These four guidelines on public library collections, if implemented will help to create balanced and useful library collections. Especially the guideline 4 emphasizes that 60% of the library budget should be spent on collection development. This guideline is not presently practiced by public libraries especially in Andhra Pradesh where a network of public libraries are functioning in the State under Zilla Grandhalaya Samasthas (NGSs).

KINDS OF SERVICES

In appendix 6, the WG identified seven types of services to be provided by all types of libraries. It has also identified among the seventeen services, four basic services viz.

1. Lending material for home use,
2. Reading facilities,
3. Reference Service, and
4. Providing Internet Access.

The other services include Inter-Library Loan, Photo-Copying, Extension Services, Document Delivery, Community Information Services, OPAC, User Education, Websites, Portals, and Institutional Repositories.

In addition to the above 'routine' library services, the WG identified the following "new and imaginative services" to be performed by the libraries:

1. Book discussion groups,

2. Lectures and discussions on subjects that effect local citizens,
3. Cultural programmes,
4. Celebrations of important events,
5. Help to prepare competitive examinations and
6. IT training at different levels.

Comment

Some of these services are being performed by the public libraries at different levels especially in Andhra Pradesh with a degree of difference. As far as the introduction of Information and Communication Technologies, most of the Public Libraries are lagging behind. Especially in the provision of OPAC and launching of Websites, portals, subject gateways, digitization of rare resources (with few exceptions) most of the public libraries in the State and elsewhere are lagging behind. This may be due to lack of proper infrastructure, trained manpower, required finances and lack of support from the Government.

ACCESS TO COLLECTIONS

The WG in appendix 8, identified four "access mechanisms' which include:

1. Collection organization and integrated access,
2. Infrastructure requirements for cataloging, data base creation and networking,
3. Networking of public libraries and
4. National Repository of Bibliographic Records.

Comment

With regards to local access, the WG recommended the use of latest Information and Communication Technologies (ICT) by all types of libraries. Especially in public libraries the use ICT is not encouraging. The application of ICT in the public library system in Andhra Pradesh is not encouraging. In most of the District Central Libraries we find still card catalogues. There is no proper system of classification and cataloging. With regards to effective local access, the situation is not that encouraging. For effective local access the public library system in A. P. has to go a longway.

As regards networking of public libraries the WG estimated 54,000 public libraries 'in existence' in the Country and they should be networked in a phased manner. The WG identified three phases to be undertaken by DELNET and INFLIBNET supported by RRRLF and project should be completed by 2011.

It is not clear on what basis the WG had estimated that there exist 54,000 public libraries in the country. The figure may not be correct. Will it be possible for the entrusting bodies such as DELNET and INFLIBNET to complete the working of networking by 2011? What is the fate of National Knowledge Commission's recommendations?

STAFFING PATTERN AND STAFF REQUIREMENT OF LIBRARIES

The WG in appendix 10 identified the staffing pattern for various types of libraries including public libraries. As far public libraries, the WG identified four categories of public libraries viz: *1. State Central Library, 2. District Library, 3. Sub-divisional / town library and 4. Rural Knowledge Centre / Community Information Centre. It has also listed various types of activities to be performed by these four categories of libraries. The WG has also recommended the following staff structure:* 1. Managerial (Group-A), 2. Professional / Technical Staff (Group-B) and 3. Para-Professional / Support Staff (Group-C). It has also recommended the provision of administrative staff such as: Night watchman, Cleaner, Mali, Driver, Book Binder, Sweeper, etc. and these are to be outsourced.

Comment

It appears that recommending three categories of staff for various types of public libraries working at different levels, for example in Andhra Pradesh, is over simplification and far from ground realities. The WG did not recommend the staffing requirements for various types of public libraries keeping in view the objectives, functions, collections, services rendered and the geographical area covered by a public library. It appears that the WG failed to take into consideration the ground realities obtaining especially in those States where public library law is in operation and where a network of public libraries are functioning at different levels and the, staffing pattern being followed for rendering various types of public library services.

The WG simply identified the three to four categories of structure but did not laid the standards for staff requirements depending upon the size of collections, services rendered and the geographical area to be covered by the public libraries. It appears that the WG has not taken into consideration the present scenario obtaining in the States where library legislation is in vogue and the public library system came in to being as a result of library legislation.

POSSIBLE IMPACT ON PUBLIC LIBRARY SERVICES

As stated already, the WG has made in all twenty nine (29) recommendations broadly covering:

1. LIS Policy,
2. Finance,
3. Library Management,
4. Access and Networking,
5. Private Collections,
6. Digitization and Open Access,
7. Staffing and
8. Public and private partnership.

These recommendations meant for all types of libraries and there were no specific recommendations for public libraries as such. Some of the recommendation may have some impact on the development of Public libraries and their services if implemented right earnestly and quickly by the Central and State Governments in the Country. The possible impact of some of the recommendations are briefly presented in the succeeding paras.

LIS POLICY

The WG under LIS policy has recommended that "Libraries should be included in the 'Concurrent List' of the Constitution of India by an Act of Parliament". If this recommendation is implemented especially the 'public libraries' which is currently in 'Sate subjects' may get central governments financial support for accelerated development and better services for the user community. But the reactions of the State Governments for this recommendation need to be assessed.

The WG has also recommended for the appointment of 'National Commission on Libraries' on a permanent basis. This is long overdue as there is, so far, no national commission for libraries. Once the Commission is set up, public libraries, perhaps, may receive the attention of the National Commission for the growth and development of public libraries and services through out the country.

FINANCE

The WG has recommended that "a specific percentage of the Central and State Education budgets must be earmarked for libraries". It further recommended that a 'Central Library Finance' should be instituted to take care of existing libraries over a period of 3 - 5 years. If this recommendation is accepted by Central and State Governments, public libraries may get required finances for offering better services to the community at large. They may be in a position to offer some of the services listed by the WG in Table-2 to Appendix-6.

LIBRARY MANAGEMENT

The WG in one of its recommendation stated that "Public Libraries must be run by local self government through committees of civil society representing the users of the library". This recommendation has certain implications to the existing pattern of public libraries functioning in those States where library legislation is in operation for decades. For example in Andhra Pradesh, the Zilla Grandhalaya Samsthas (ZGS) were managing public libraries in the rural and urban areas in the district.

It appears that the WG has not given due thought to this aspect while making this specific recommendation especially for public libraries.

ACCESS AND NETWORKING

Networking helps for optimum utilization existing resources to offer better services to the user community especially in rural areas. The WG recommended for networking of Public Libraries in phased manner and to be completed within five years. In appendix-8 the manner in which the work should be carried out was outlined and emphasized the need for adapting state of the art technology for the said purpose.

This is a stupendous task of networking 54,000 public libraries in the country as estimated by the WG. The WG set 2011 as the deadline for completion of the work. Is it possible to complete the work by 2011 even if the recommendations are accepted by the Central Government and tries to implement them right earnest.

CONCLUSION

The appointment of National Knowledge Commission (NKC) by the Government of India is a landmark in the realization of Indian Society transforming itself into truly knowledge society. The recommendation of WG on libraries set up by NKC, if implement at the earliest will transform the library scenario in the Country and public libraries as Gateways to Knowledge".

The implications of recommendations of NKC are far reaching especially on public library services. The Central and State Governments concerned have to right earnestly work in random to implement the recommendations with necessary financial support so as to enable the public libraries in the Country to offer effective and wholesome information / knowledge services to the user communities especially in rural areas. The fate of recommendations of earlier committees / commissions should not fall on the recommendations of NKC. It is not know clearly the present status of NKC and the WG on libraries. It is also not known the response of the State Governments towards the recommendations of NKC. Let us hope for better days for public library development in the Country.

Source Document

Libraries: Gateways to Knowledge: A Roadmap for Revitalization. New Delhi, National Knowledge Commission, 2007.

Facet 2

LIBRARY CLASSIFICATION

3

Library Classification: An International Perspective

INTRODUCTION

The history of modern library classification (LC) can be traced from the epoch making year of 1876 when Melvil Dewey published his now world famous Decimal Classification. During the past twelve decades major developments and trends have taken place in the growth and development of LC giving it an International perspective when compared to other traditional branches of Library Science such as Cataloging, Indexing, Abstracting. S. R. Ranganathan has very lucidly presented a century of classification and recognized three distinct periods in its growth and development during the past one hundred years i.e. 1876-1975.

These are: 1. Pre-facet period (1876-1896); 2. Transition to Facet period (1897-1932); 3. Facet period (1933-1975)[1].

It was during the Facet and Post-Facet period i.e. from 1975 onwards that LC attained international perspective, wherein various aspects of LC become topics for discussion at several International Conferences organized by Inter-governmental and non-governmental agencies like UNESCO, FID/CR, ISKO, and also other regional and national agencies interested in the growth and development of LC as a discipline and tool for organizing knowledge/Information in Libraries and Information Centers.[2]

The thrust of this paper is to present briefly the exposition and discussion of various facets of LC at several international conferences, which have greatly contributed to the attainment of LC as a discipline of International importance and significance and its role in the emerging Information Society.

INTERNATIONAL CONFERENCES:

During the past four decades i.e. to be specific from 1957 and onwards six International Conferences on Classification Research organized by FID/CR and four International Conferences by International Society for Knowledge Organisation (ISKO) were held besides numerous national and regional conferences. The following sections briefly deal with these Conferences.

First International Study Conference on Classification for Information Retrieval (1957)

The first International Study Conference on Classification for Information Retrieval was held at Dorking, England during 13-17 May 1957. About thirty six delegates representing eight countries including India participated in this first Conference. Ranganathan in his opening address dwelt upon "Library Classification as a discipline". The major recommendations of this first Conference touched upon: 1. Scope of Classification, 2. Schemes of Classification, 3. Need for research, 4. Use of Classification Schemes, 5. Differences between systems, 6. Construction and application of schemes, 7. Notation for such visually scanned systems as the card catalogue, 8. Machine systems, 9. Research Projects, 10. A general scheme for classification, 11. Development of Classification Schemes and 12. Furtherance of research.

International study Conference on Classification Research (1964)

After seven years of the first conference, the second International Study Conference on Classification Research was held at Elsinore, Denmark during 14-18 September, 1964. Fifty seven delegates and six observes representing fifteen countries and two international bodies attended this Conference. S. R. Ranganathan delivered the Presidential address entitled "Library Classification through a century" . The papers presented and discussed in this Conference were grouped into five areas: 1. General theory of classification, 2. Research in mechanized classification, 3. Selected and Special Schemes, 4. Evaluation Techniques and 5. Directions for future work. 5

Third International Study Conference on Classification Research (1975)

After eleven years of the second Conference, the third International Study Conference on Classification Research was held at Bombay during 6-11 January 1975. Fifty four delegates and sixty seven observers representing seven countries attended this Conference. The recommendations of this Conference were centered around: 1. General aspects of designing ordering systems for global information networks, 2. Use of empirical methods and theoretical models for designing ordering systems for global information networks, 3. Systems evaluation, 4. Inter disciplinary contacts, 5. Education and 6. Needs and problems of developing countries. In this Conference I. Dahlberg presented her reflection on the meeting.

Fourth, International Study Conference on Classification Research (1982)

After seven years of the third Conference, the fourth International Study Conference on Classification Research was held at Augsburg, Federal Republic of Germany during 28th June-2nd July 1982. The theme of the Conference was "Universal classification, subject analysis and ordering systems."[7]

Fifth International Study Conference on Classification Research (1991)

After nine years of the fourth Conference, the fifth

International Study Conference on Classification Research was held at Toronto, Canada, during June 24-28, 1991. The Conference was attended by fifty five participants from ten countries including representatives from six classification research organizations from North America and Europe. The theme of this Conference was "Classification Research for knowledge Representation and Organisation". The forty papers presented in this Conference fell into three broad categories: 1. General principles and policies, 2. Structure and Logic Classification and 3. Empirical Investigation.

Eric de Grolier who had the distinction of participating all the five FID/CR study Conferences presented a Summary and Conclusion. At the end of his presentation, de Grolier proposed recommendations for determining 'Fields in need of New Studies'. He stated that research is needed into: 1. The most efficient use of new technologies, 2. The construction of practical tools serving as bridges between different systems, 3. The means of avoiding ethnocentrism, 4. The integration of classification and terminology research, 5. The relations of classification with logico-mathematical models and numerical taxonomy, and 6. The study of notational systems. 8

Sixth, International Study Conference on Classification Research (1997)

The sixth International Study Conference on Classification Research will be held at University College, London from 16-19 June 1997 on the topic "Knowledge organisation for Information Retrieval". This is being organized by FID/CR and University College, London in association with ASLIB, the Classification Research Group (CRG) and the International Society for Knowledge Organisation (ISKO).

The themes that the sixth International Conference will explore include: 1. The role of Classification in Information Management, 2. Classification research for retrieval of information published electronically, 3. Automatic methods of Classification, 4. The Researcher and the real world, 5. Tools for classification and Classification as a tool and 6. Data modeling.[9]

INTERNATIONAL SOCIETY FOR KNOWLEDGE ORGANISATION (ISKO)

The founding of International Society for knowledge Organisation (ISKO) in 1989 was a landmark for the growth and development of classificatory thought at the international level. The main purpose is to function both on a national and international levels as a connecting link between any and all institutions concerned with conceptual questions pertaining to the organisation and processing of knowledge. It wishes to intensify and accelerate exchange of experience thereby help to fill a wide spread need for classification and expansion of existing knowledge in the domain of classification.

ISKO has set before itself the following tasks: 1. Promotion of research, development and application of all methods for the organisation of knowledge in general or of particular fields by integrating especially the conceptual approaches of classification research and artificial intelligence, 2. Awaken and support an understanding for the practical and heuristic usefulness of such an organisation of knowledge, 3. Promote on a national and international level the exchange of information and experience of scientists and practitioners, 4. Observe internationally the progress made in this work, 5. Concentrate on major points of this knowledge field in special working groups and 6. Hold regular meetings in order to support these activities.[10]

In consonance with the last task, ISKO has been organizing International Conferences biennially to promote research, development and application of methods in knowledge organisation.

First International ISKO Conference (1990)

The first International ISKO Conference was held at Darmstadt, Technical University (Germany) August 14-17, 1990. The topic chosen was "Tools for knowledge organisation and Human Interface". The Conference was co-sponsored by the German ISKO Chapter and FID/CR.

There was an impressive gathering of about 200 experts representing twenty three countries. The Conference wàs divided into twelve plenary sessions and 12 workshops. In all about 60 papers were prevented and discussed covering areas: 1. General Issues pertaining to Knowledge organisation, 2. Algorithmic text analysis, 3. Terminology, 4. Knowledge Organisation in Universal systems, 5. Thesaurus issues, 6. Online retrieval — role of classification, 7. Knowledge organisation in special systems, 8. Retrieval from Universal systems, 9. Retrieval technologies and 10. Indexing.[11]

The deliberations were extensive and fruitful. The first Conference drew scholars of outstanding merit as well as new breed of practioners of hard and software, library administrators, teachers and researchers and information consultants.

Second International ISKO Conference (1992)

The second International ISKO Conference was held in Madras (India) from August 26-28, 1992. It was sponsored by the Madras Library Association, the University of Madras and the Sarada Ranganathan Endowment for Library Science. The Conference was attended by seventy one delegates from twelve countries. The theme of the Conference was "Cognitive Paradigms in Knowledge Organisation". The papers presented at this Conference were grouped into the following broad categories. 1. Knowledge and knowledge organisation: The needs and modes, 2. Knowledge seeking in Libraries, 3. Knowledge seeking in Information Retrieval, 4. Knowledge seeking in problem solving, decision making and learning situations, 5. Taxonomic approach to knowledge organisation, 6. Analytico-synthetic approaches knowledge organisation, 7.

Cognitive paradigms and their application to knowledge organisation and 8. Cognitive paradigms in knowledge bases.

Third International ISKO Conference (1994)

The third International ISKO Conference was held at the

Royal School of Librarianship Copenhagen, Denmark, June 21-24, 1994. The theme of the Conference was "Knowledge Organisation and Quality Management". Fifty six papers were presented on the following eight major topical areas: 1. Quality in knowledge organisation, 2. Theory of knowledge organisation, 3. Future prospects for Classification Schemes and Thesauri, 4. Knowledge organisation in specific domains, 5. Concept representation in Systems Design, 6. Linguistics in Knowledge Organisation, 7. Communication and Knowledge Organisation. 8. New Technologies and Knowledge Organisation.[13]

Fourth International ISKO Conference (1996)

The fourth International ISKO Conference was held in James Madison Memorial Building, Library of Congress, Washington (USA) July 15-19, 1996. The main theme of the Conference was "Knowledge organisation and change". The sub-themes on which experts presented papers were: 1. Library of Congress Classification, 2. Management of Change in Knowledge Organisation, 3. Knowledge organisation in cross-cultural and cross-linguistic settings, 4. Role of Relationships in Knowledge Organisation, 5. Knowledge organisation in the online Environment, 6. Impact of Technologies on Bibliographic Elements, 7. Knowledge Organisation in the Economic Environment, 8. User Focus in knowledge Organisation, 9. Thesauri and Metathesauri, 10. Knowledge Organisation and Images, 11. Inter play of Epistemology and Knowledge Organisation, 12. Inter disciplinary approaches to knowledge organisation, 13. Natural Language Processing and 14. Dewey Decimal Classification.

CONCLUSION

The six FID/CR International Study Conferences on Classification Research and the proposed sixth Conference in 1997 to be organized by FID/CR and the four International ISKO Conferences held so far clearly demonstrated that Library Classification/Knowledge organisation will have greater relevance, importance and role to play, in the he years to come in the context of emerging Information Technology. Library Classification/ Knowledge Organisation shall remain as the main focus of attention and discussion at International forai thanks to the concerted efforts made by FID/CR and ISKO in this direction. Needless to state that no other branch of Library & Information Science has reached such new heights at the internal level than Library Classification/Knowledge organisation. Thanks to the vision and contributions of Ranganathan, who laid strong foundations for the growth and development of Library Classification as a discipline of par excellence in the field of Library and Information Science and now transforming into knowledge organisation and becoming an important theme/aspect for discussion at International Conferences, Seminars and Workshops. The preceding sections present a perspective picture of Library Classification/knowledge organisation at the International level.

REFERENCES

1. Ranganathan, S.R. Library Classification through a century. Library Science. V2, N1, 1965, pp.1-30.
2. Raju, A.A.N. Decimal, Universal Decimal and Colon classification; a study in comparison. Delhi, Ajanta Publications, 1984. pp. 257-270.
3. Ranganathan, S.R., Library Classification as a discipline. In International Conference on Classification for Information Retrieval. Proceedings. London, ASLIB, 1957.
4. Ranganathan, S.R., Library Classification through a Century. op.cit.
5. Atherton, P. Ed. The Second International Study Conference on Classification Research. Proceedings. Copenhagen, Munksguard, 1965.
6. FID/CR News. *International Classification*, V2, No.1, May 75, pp.37-44.
7. FID Newsletter on Education and Training Programs for Specialized Information Personnel. V4, N1, Spring 1982.
8. FID/CR News 30. The ICSSR Conference. *International Classification*. V18, N4, 1991, pp.229-232.
9. Reports and Communications. 6th International Study Conference on Classification Research. *Knowledge Organisation*. V23, N2, 1996. p.107.
10. ISKO. *International Classification*, V16, N3/4, 1989.

11. Satija, M.P. Tools for Knowledge Organisation and Human Interface. Report of the first ISKO Conference. *International Classification.* V17, N3/4, 1990. pp.169-176.
12. Gopinath, M.A. Congnitive Paradigms in Knowledge- Organisation. Technical Report on the 2nd international ISKO Conference. *International Classification.* V19, N4, 1992. pp.217-222.
13. Knowledge organisation and Quality Management. 3rd International ISKO Conference, Copenhagen. *Knowledge Organisation,* V21, N1, 1994. pp.38-40.
14. ISKO Fourth International Conference, Program. *Knowledge Organisation.* V23, N1, 1996. pp.31-33.

4

Universal Decimal Classification (UDC): Features And Developments

INTRODUCTION

UDC is one of the most important general schemes of library classification. The scheme was developed on the basis of Decimal Classification and first published in 1905 entitled *Classification Decimale Vniverselle* by Paul Otlet and Henri La Fontaine. The scheme is updated and revised from time to time by International Federation for Information and Documentation (FID). The scheme is very widely and extensively used in most of the special libraries and information centres and also by bibliographical services throughout the world.

DIFFERENT EDITIONS OF UDC

The second complete edition of UDC in French was published during the years 1927-1933. In 1934, the third full edition in German entitled *"Dezimal Klassification"* was begun and completed in 1952. The British Standards Institution (BSI) took responsibility for the publication of UDC in English. It began in 1943 the publication of 4th edition and completed it in 1977. It constitutes a British Standard BS 1000.

Abridged Editions in English

In addition to above mentioned full editions, abridged editions of the whole UDC have been published in 13 different languages. The first English abridged edition was published in 1948, the second edition in 1957 and the third edition in 1961. The multilingual edition BS 1000B in German, English and French was published in 1958.

In order to meet the changing needs of LICs and at an affordable price, the International Medium Edition (IME) English text was brought out by BSI in 1985 (BSI 1000M: (1985) in two parts, viz., Part 1: Systematic Tables (1985) and Part 2: Alphabetical Subject Index (1988). Another IME was published in 1993.

In addition to various signs and symbols already provided in AEE, two more new symbols:

→ (arrow) meaning 'see also';

e.g., 159.9 Psychology

→ 301.155, 591.51, 612.821, 616.89; and

≅ (parallel division) meaning 'subdivision as' have been introduced in 1985 IME edition.

e.g., 611.3 Digestive System, Alimentary Canal

611.3 ≅ 616.3, e.g. 611.31. Oral Cavity Mouth

Management of UDC

For many years, UDC was managed by FID. On January 1, 1992 all rights in UDC were transferred to UDC Consortium (UDCC) of which FID was founder member along with five UDC publishers including BSI.

Master Reference File (MRF)

The Central Secretariat of the UDCC maintains the Master Reference File, the data base of 60,000 entries which is the authoritative statement of the content of UDC. The MRF will be the authority for and source of published UDC editions and the second edition of BSI 1000M is the first product from this source.

The official language of UDCC is English; class descriptors in the data base are currently in English but it is planned to extend to include French and German.

BSI is the publisher of English language editions.

Revision of UDC

The scheme is under continuous revision. An Editor-in-Chief has been appointed and will be supported by an editorial board to maintain the quality of UDC and enhance its international credibility.

The revision proposals are now being published in *Extensions and Corrections* which was started in 1933. Since 1949 it became a journal publication entitled *"Extensions and Corrections to the UDC"*. This was at first semi-annual and later annual cumulating in 3 year series.

Common Auxiliary Tables

- la Coordination. Extension
- 1b Relation. Subgrouping. Order-fixing
- 1c Language
- 1d Form
- 1e Place
- 1f Ethnic grouping and nationality
- 1g Time
- 1h Subject specification by notations from non-UDC sources
- 1i Point of view
- 1k General characteristics.
  Materials, Persons

STRUCTURE OF UDC

In UDC we find two kinds of tables, viz., the main schedules and auxiliary tables which include common and special. The auxiliary tables support the main structure, i.e., the schedules for the classification of compound subjects. The schedules of various main classes reflect the enumerative nature of the scheme. The auxiliaries contribute to the synthetic nature of the scheme. The following schematic representation provides a clear picture of the structure of UDC:

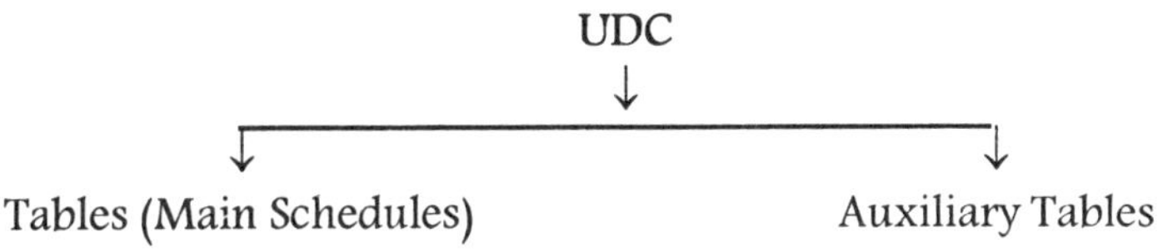

AUXILIARY TABLES

The most innovative and significant feature in UDC is its auxiliary notation consisting of signs and sub-divisions which greatly contributed to synthetic nature of UDC. The auxiliary notation in UDC is of two kinds — common and special. The following chart depicts the variety of these auxiliaries. In IME we notice certain changes in respect of scope, coverage, enumeration and terminology used in various types of these auxiliaries.

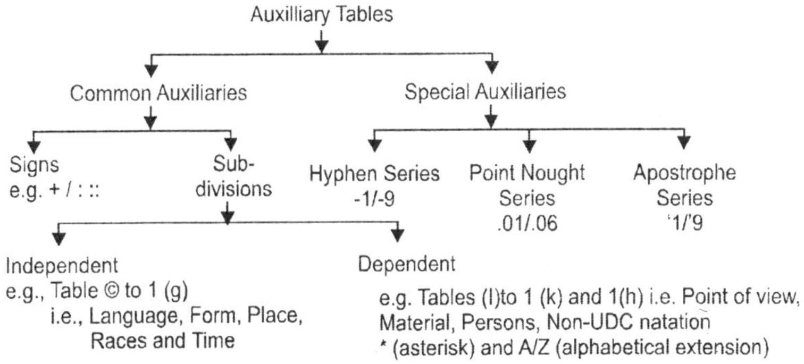

Common Auxiliaries

The common auxiliaries denote recurring ideas/concepts and applicable throughout the scheme. These have greatly enhanced the synthetic nature of the scheme and help us in variety of ways for number building.

Special Auxiliaries

The special auxiliaries denote locally recurrent ideas/ concepts and are applicable in limited or restricted range of the schedules. In other words these can be used for few main classes and not for all main classes in the scheme.

Common Auxiliaries Signs (Tables 1(a) - 1(b))

The common auxiliary signs are: + (plus), / (stroke),: (colon), [ ] (square brackets) and :: (double colon) which serve as relators for synthesising UDC numbers. These signs have different functions to perform. The + plus and / stroke are used to represent aggregation. The : colon is a most dominant and powerful sign in UDC. This sign is used to represent various types of relations. The sign colon is used in EVE to indicate a simple relation and also to indicate sub-grouping and order-fixing with associate signs [ ] square brackets and :: double colon respectively.

Examples

Table 1(a) Coordination and Extension + /

Introduction to Knowledge, Metaphysics and Logic 00 + 11 + 16

Mechanics 531/534

Table 1(b) Relation, Grouping, Order-fixing : \ 1 ::

Influence of Politics on Education 37:32

Science and Technology in India [5+6] (540)

International Federation of Library Associations and Institutions (IFLA)

061.2(100)::02IFLA

Common Auxiliary Subdivisions

These consist of numerical tables in which common concepts are enumerated and arranged hierarchically. These fall into two groups, viz., Independent and Dependent auxiliaries.

Independent Auxiliaries

These tables may be attached to any UDC notation wherever

necessary or may be used on their own to form compound class number. These are tables l(c) — l(g) the auxiliaries of Language Table l(c), Form l(d), Place l(e), Race l(f) and Time l(g).

Examples

Table l(c) Language = equals

Dictionary of Banking Industry in India in English 664.6(540)(058)=20

Table 1(d) Form (0...) brackets nought

Encyclopedia of Biology 57(031)

Table l(e) Place 1/9 in brackets

Political Parties in India 329(540)

Table l(f) Race and Nationality (=...) brackets equals

Birth Customs of Jews 392.12(=924)

Common Auxiliaries of Time " " double quotation marks

Social and Political Conditions in India During 7th Century 308(540)"06"

Dependent Auxiliaries

The dependent auxiliary tables have to be necessarily attached to a UDC class number. These are specified in tables l(i) and l(k). The point of view auxiliaries are listed in table l(i) and common auxiliaries of materials and persons are listed in table l(k). The table l(h) specification by non-UDC notation is also dependent for all practical purposes as the symbols * asterisk and A/Z Roman capital letters have to be attached to UDC number.

Examples

Table l(h) Specification by Non-UDC Notation

Indian National Highway 6 625.711.1(540)*6

Hindustan Machine Tools 621.9:061.5(540)HMT

Table 1(i) Point of View .00 point nought nought

Art from Metaphysical Point of View 7.000.11

New Dependent Auxiliary Tables

The IME (1985 and 1993) provide for new tables of common auxiliaries of Materials Table l(k)-03 and Persons Table l(k)-05. These two new tables have further strengthened the synthetic nature of UDC.

Examples

Morocco Leather Book Binding 686.1-035.513

Skilled Workers in Colour Industries 667-057.21

Special Auxiliary Subdivisions

There are no major changes affected in IME editions in respect of three types of special auxiliaries, viz., a) hyphen series -1/-9, point nought series .01/.09 and apostrophe series '1/'9. The application of these three series is stated in the schedules with clarity and examples.

Examples

Epic Poems in Sanskrit 891.2-13

Animal Life in Painting 75.042

Sodium Chloride 546.33'131

IMPORTANT CHANGES

The most important change affected in IME 1985 is keeping the main class 4 Philology, Linguistics, Languages vacant. In other words, the digit 4 has been frozen. The main class Linguistics and its subdivisions have been transferred to main class 80 Linguistics, Philology and Languages.

Another important change incorporated in the schedules under each main class and its divisions is to clearly indicate the special auxiliary divisions and principal divisions of a main class.

Parallel Divisions

Another important innovation introduced in IME is parallel division device indicated by the symbol ≅ at various points in the schedules. This device results in the same notation being used to denote a given concept in more than one place. This device means that the number preceding ≅ may be sub-divided in a manner analogous to the number following it. A simple example is:

294.11 Vedism

294.11 ≅ 291

e.g., 294.112.14 Gods: Indra, Agni (from 291.214)

Intercalation

Intercalation has been defined as "the use of an auxiliary as an infix rather than a prefix or suffix". The implication of this device is that certain auxiliaries may interrupt a main number creating a compound class number.

e.g.	622.343	Copper Mining
	622(540).343	Mining - India - Copper

Alphabetical Subject Index

Part 2 of IME93 is the Alphabetical Subject Index. This is a computer generated index. The entries in the index reflect the terminology used in the schedules. The arrangement of entries in the index is word-by-word. Here is a simple entry from the index:

Lighters	629.123.15,662.58
cigar and cigarette	662.592
electric	662.558
flint	662.592
pocket	662.59
using solar heat	662.591

DEVELOPMENTS IN UDC

UDC in Computer-based Information Retrieval Systems

It was suggested as far as back as in 1934 that UDC was suitable for 'mechanical sorting'. The Royal Society's Scientific Information Conference held in 1945 noted the need to explore the potentialities of UDC in mechanised retrieval. The research programmes carried out in US, Britain, Germany, Denmark and Switzerland in the sixties helped UDC to be usable as indexing language for computerised control and processing of information in the fields of knowledge. The most significant research work in this respect was American Institute of Physics' UDC Project under Freeman and Atherton. Other experiments carried out during the late sixties in using UDC for special mechanical applications include, for example, the indexing of *Geo-Science Abstracts* and the maintenance of user profiles in the metallurgic field.

UDC and UNISIST

FID thought of making UDC as 'Roof Scheme' under which it could be hung the relevant special classifications, thesauri or descriptor lists as well as the more detailed UDC divisions themselves for those who prefer a homogeneous UDC-based system. The concept received encouragement in the efforts to make UDC adopted as switching language for UNISIST (United Nations World Science Information System), the joint project of ICSU/ UNESCO. An ASLIB study for the UNISIST stated that UDC was found 'least unsatisfactory' of the major existing schemes.

Computerisation of the UDC

For more than three decades UDC has been used advantageously in computerised bibliographical and abstracting services mostly for the production of subject indexes but also for information retrieval and SDI. In the forefront of UDC mechanisation has been Rugby, who as early as in 1964 showed the Conference at Elsinore the printout of *Meteorological and Geoastrophysical Titles* that had started the use of the computer for author and subject indexing. A more comprehensive survey on the use of computers with the UDC was compiled by Rigby with the description of more than sixty experimental or operational systems in fifteen countries and four international projects.

CONCLUSION

In order to meet the growing needs of LICs, especially classification of microdocuments, library classification schemes have to be revised at regular intervals. Keeping this fact in view, FID brought out IMEs in 1985 and 1993. These medium editions contain about a third of the material of the full edition. The fME 1993 has greatly increased the scope of many subjects by introducing minute divisions to achieve co-extensive class numbers. Thus UDC 1ME93 has become an efficient tool for organisation and retrieval of information in LICs.

SUGGESTED READINGS

Raju, A.A.N. *UDC IME, 1985; a practical and self instructional manual.* Madras, T.R. Publications, 1991.

UDC IME, 1993. London, BSI, 1993.

5

Fine Arts: Scope and Treatment in the Universal Decimal Classification and Colon Classification

INTRODUCTION

Humanities are some of the important branches of Universe of Knowledge. The scholars and authoritative reference sources differ widely in identifying the scope of Humanities. For example; *Encyclopaedia Americana*[1] defined Humanities as "branches of learning that deal with human thought and culture excluding the Sciences. The term was applied originally to the study of literatures of classical Greece and Rome. It has since been expanded to cover all languages and literatures, the arts, history and philosophy."

Humanities are considered to constitute a distinct branch of Universe of Knowledge, which emphasise the human values and expression of the spirit of man. The above two definitions agreed to include the arts as one of the branches of Humanities even though there is a divergence with regards to other branches some of which may fall under Social Sciences.

DEFINITION AND SCOPE

The term 'Arts' is applied to a realm so vast and indefinite as to include literature, music and dance, theatre, films, the visual and decorative arts and other equally diverse activities.[2] Sometimes the terms Humanities and Arts are used synonymously. The realm of 'Arts' is classified into seven overlapping groups, viz. 1. Useful Arts, 2. Fine Arts, 3. Lesser Arts, 4. Decorative Arts, 5. Social, Civil and Religious Arts, 6. Sportive Arts, and 7. Cosmic Arts.[3] There is even no agreement on this broad classification. The various sub-branches of these seven broad fields overlap on one another. Fine Arts have been defined as "the powerful expression and deep appreciation of values of human life, such expressions taking the forms of the play, dancing, drama, drawing, painting, sculpture, architecture, literary pursuits (prose & poetry) and music using the finer, more developed techniques of line, colour, form, tone and words giving rise to institutions, developing and encouraging them."[4]

INDIAN TRADITION

According to Indian tradition, Arts have been classified on the basis of sensory experience. Those Arts which are concerned with the sensory organ eye, are designated as Visual Arts and those concerned with auditory organ car arc Auditory Arts. There are certain Arts which come under both the categories, and these are designated as 'Audiovisual Arts.' As per the Indian tradition, there are sixty-four Arts which fall under the three groups viz. Visual, Audio and Audio-visual. There is no agreement about the listing of these sixty-four arts in the authoritative Indian sources of information. Vignana Sarvasvam[6] (Telugu Encyclopaedia) listed the sixty-four arts taken from *Grandha Sanjna Darpanam,* an authoritative Sanskrit work. These sixty-four Arts are broadly based on *Rasa* and utility. Those Arts which are based on *Rasa* are designated as Fine Arts and those based on utility are designated as Useful Arts.

WESTERN INFLUENCE

The meaning, scope, relevance, utility and understanding of these sixty-four arts have been changing as a consequence to changing times and needs of societies. The Western concept of Arts, especially Fine Arts has a greater influence on the literature that is being published on various aspects of Fine Arts. The institutions of higher learning, especially the universities, academies, learned institutions and societies concerned with Fine Arts—teaching, development and practice—reflect this Western conception and division of Fine Arts. The universal classification schemes also do reflect this Western classification of Fine Arts. The following sections briefly deal with the treatment of Fine Arts in the two important universal schemes for classification, viz. 1. Universal Decimal Classification (UDC, IME, 1985) and Colon Classification (CC 7lh edn., 1987).

IMPORTANT BRANCHES

The most important branches of fine arts, viz. Architecture, Sculpture, Painting, Music, Dance have been given fair treatment in both the universal schemes for classification, viz. UDC (IME, 1985) and CC (7th edn.). Various sub-branches of these Fine Arts have been taken care of by both the schemes. UDC at the beginning of the schedule for Fine Arts, has provided a special auxiliary schedules, which can be applied to all the Fine Arts, with exception to 77 (Photography). With the help of this special auxiliary sub-divisions, viz. aesthetics, philosophy 01, technique 02, periods and phases 03, subjects for artistic representation 04, application of art 05, plagiarism 061, occupations and activities 07, characteristic features, forms 08, performance presentation 091, various aspects of fine arts can be represented in the class number. The provision of various branches of Fine Arts and their sub-branches in UDC is shown in the Annexure I.

The provision and scope of various branches of Fine Arts has greatly been increased in the 7th edn. of CC. In the 6th edition we could find 22 Fine Arts and the number has been increased to

32 in the 7th edition of CC. With exception of few important branches of Fine Arts, viz. Numismatic Art N29, Drawing N5, Painting N6, Engraving N7, Architecture NA, Furniture NA, Town Planning NB, Plastic Art NC, Sculpture ND, Inlay Art NJ, and Music NR; the rest of the Fine Arts have not been provided with detailed schedules i.e. special isolates. The schedule of basic subjects in Fine Arts may help to assign broad class numbers but is not of any help for depth classification. The schedule of basic subjects in CC with corresponding UDC (IME, 1985) class numbers is shown in Annexure 2.

PROBLEMS OF CLASSIFICATION

The two Universal Schemes have made no attempt at fundamental classifications of Fine Arts, the listing more often than not reflecting notational convenience. This is more evident in the UDC. The Arts main class in UDC includes all the sports, entertainments and of course all the major Fine Arts. CC has greatly expanded the list of basic subjects falling under Fine Arts. But sports and entertainment have been put under the main class M, Useful Arts.

Langridge[7] has identified the major problems in the classification of all branches of arts including fine arts. The main problem being the distinction between the products of the discipline itself and the writings about those products. The other problems are various aspects and points of view represented and studied in the Fine Arts, identification and treatment of individual artists and their works, specifying period divisions of various Fine Arts, and cultural traditions and styles of Fine Arts emanating from various countries.

INDIVIDUAL ARTISTS AND THEIR WORKS

In Colon Classification through classic device (CLD), individual artists and their works, if they arc classics falling under various branches of Fine Arts, can be classified. With the help of this device different editions of a classic including commentaries and translations can be brought together. In the 6th edition of CC (1963), part-3 is devoted to schedules of classics and sacred books with special names. Some of the classics from Architecture, Music and Dance arc also listed in this part.

UDC (IME, 1985) provides Alphabetical Device (AD) A/Z to represent proper names, abbreviations and acronyms. At the beginning of the main class 7, the Arts, we find this direction "7 ... A/Z, works of particular artists or practitioners." This device has been mentioned at various places in schedules for the main class 7. For example at 75 (Page 470) we could notice "75 A/Z, Works of named painters, e.g. 75 Rubens, works of Rubens." This way we can represent works of individual artists or practitioners. We can also notice another important provision at the beginning of the main class 7 for representing "7-05 persons and personal characteristics in the arts etc." This is to be extended by Table 1(K) i.e. Common Auxiliaries of Persons and Personal Characteristics. With the help of these provisions various aspects of persons concerned with various branches of Fine Arts can be classified.

SCHOOLS, STYLES AND PERIODS

In CC, to represent different styles in Fine Arts, Geographical Device (GD) and Chronological Devices (CD) have been employed. The resulting number should be enclosed in circular brackets. The symbol for Fine Arts N is to be divided by (GD) and (CD). For example N (44, J), Moghul Painting; NA (41), Chinese Architecture, NT (58, N), Modem Russian Theatre. This device will greatly help in classifying various schools and styles, periods in printing.

UDC, at the beginning of the schedule for Fine Arts listed a variety of special auxiliary divisions which can be applied to all the branches of Fine Arts with exception to 77, Photography. The periods and phases, schools, styles and influences are listed under the special auxiliary 7.03. The special auxiliary division, 7.03 is minutely divided to include .031, Prehistoric and Primitive Art; .032, Ancient Civilizations of the World; .033, Medieval (Christian, Islamic); .034, Renaissance; .035, post-Renaissance and .036,

Modern Art movements. At 7.033/ .035 instruction has been given to intercalate place auxiliaries from Table l(e), to achieve geographical grouping of styles, e.g. 7.033.4 (410.1)1 Anglo-Saxon Art. Different schools of Oriental Arts have been listed under 7.032.1. At 7.036, Modern Arts movements, instruction has been provided to use Tables l(c) and 1 (g) to indicate geographical and chronological groupings by intercalating space and time divisions, e.g. 7.036 (430) 7, German expressionism, 7.036 "189", Modern Art movements of the 1890s.

CAPACITY OF THE UNIVERSAL SCHEMES TO CLASSIFY LITERATURE ON FINE ARTS

The two universal schemes have built-in capacity to classify both macro as well as micro literature of various branches of Fine Arts with the help of a variety of devices, notational techniques, general and special auxiliary schedules.

COLON CLASSIFICATION (CC)

The five devices in *CC*, viz. 1. Chronological Device (CD), 2. Geographical Device (GD), 3. Subject Device (SD), 4. Alphabetical Device (AD) and 5. Enumeration Device (ED) have been greatly exploited to arrive at co-extensive class number. These devices avoid enumeration and thereby shorten an array in a schedule, give autonomy to the classifier and secure automatic conformity to the canons of classification.[8]

Classic Device

In addition to the above five devices, CC provides for classic device (CLD) to classify works of classical authors in the various branches of universe of subjects. As per this device, the classic becomes a subject by itself that is a quasi subject. Therefore, its different editions and translations come together. Not only different editions of a classic, but commentaries and sub-commentaries will come together with the host book. This type of bringing together of all related works of a classic is known as 'Classic cluster'[9]. The helpful sequence within 'Classic cluster' brought out by classic device will be very convenient and helpful to readers.

Part G of CC (7th edn.) is supposed to provide a list of about 2,000 Indian classics with their class numbers, constructed by classic device. But the said list is not found in CC (7th edn.). Perhaps this list may be included in the remaining two volumes of CC to be devoted to the index and the worked out examples.

General Divisions and Common Isolates

In addition to the different devices and a proposed schedule of classics, the list of basic subjects have been greatly increased in respect of Fine Arts in the 7th edition, when compared with 6th edition of CC (See Annexure 2). Besides these basic subjects, the detailed schedule of Common Isolates such as Energy, Matter Property, Personality, Language, Space, Time and Anteriorising Common Isolates will help the classifier to classify minute aspects falling under various branches of Fine Arts.

Besides these Common Isolates, the provision of environment divisions has greatly enhanced the capacity of CC to build co-extensive class number. With the help of these divisions we can form environmental specials by prefixing the digit 9. The environment divisions such as Chemical nature (N), Biological (NZ), Microbiological nature (P), Political, Social and Economic environment (W, X, Y), Religion Y7 (Q), will greatly help to classify literature under Fine Arts.

UNIVERSAL DECIMAL CLASSIFICATION (UDC)

UDC (IME, 1985) has provided a fairly comprehensive list of various branches of Fine Arts (See Annexure 1). The detailed schedules pertaining to various branches of Fine Arts and several types of common and special auxiliaries have enhanced the capacity of UDC for depth classification.

Special Auxiliary Subdivisions (SAS)

The special auxiliaries are not listed at one place. They occur at various places in the schedules and express concepts that are recurrent, but in a more limited subject range.[10] The provision of Special Auxiliary Subdivisions (SAS), at the beginning of the main class, Arts (7) has greatly enhanced the capacity of UDC for minute classification. The SAS 7.01-7.097, includes aspects such as aesthetics .01, technique .02, periods and phases .03, subjects for artistic representation .04, application of art .05, forgery, counterfeiting .061, occupations and activities associated with arts .07, characteristic features, forms .08, performances, presentation .091 will greatly help the classifier to represent various aspects of Fine Arts in the class number.

Besides these SAS applicable to all branches of Fine Arts except 77, at the beginning of each branch of Fine Arts we find a schedule of special auxiliaries applicable to that branch of Fine Art only. The SAS represents various aspects of fine arts which are not found in Colon Classification, 7th edition.

Common Auxiliary Subdivisions (CAS)

The provision of detailed schedule of CAS, viz. 1. Language, 2. Form, 3. Place, 4. Race and Nationality, 5. Time, 6. Point of view, 7. Materials and 8. Persons have greatly enhanced the capacity of UDC for classifying various aspects of Fine Arts. Especially, the provision of materials -03 and person -05 in the IME, 1985, is an added feature hitherto absent in the earlier abridged editions of UDC.

In some of the schedules of common auxiliaries, we could find the provision of SAS which have greatly strengthened base CAS. The SAS are more evident in Form, Place and Race and Nationality.

CONCLUSION

The preceding sections will give us an idea about the scope and treatment of Fine Arts in both the schemes and their capacity to classify micro literature falling under various branches of Fine Arts. The approach of CC with respect to Fine Arts is Oriental and that of UDC is Occidental. In CC an effort has been made to present various branches of Fine Arts based on Indian Philosophy, Culture,

Civilization and Tradition. The detailed schedule of basic subjects in Fine Arts and very elaborate schedule of Common Isolates in the 7th edition well supported by various devices and notational techniques have greatly enhanced the capacity of CC to arrive at co-extensive class number. The scheme has very clearly taken into consideration the origin and development of Fine Arts from the Indian point of view, the literary warrant had provided necessary schedules to meet the requirements of libraries especially those libraries rich in Indian Fine Arts and Indological subjects both in India and elsewhere.

The approach of UDC towards Fine Arts is western and therefore, more emphasis was laid on western concept of Fine Arts. The schedules were tailored to meet this approach. The IME, 1985 provides very comprehensive schedules for various branches of Fine Arts, well supported by several sets of special auxiliary subdivisions (SAS). In addition to these SAS, various types of Common Auxiliary Subdivisions (CAS) have enhanced the capacity of UDC to achieve minute classification and truly attained the status of a universal scheme.

For obvious reasons the scheme has not given the required emphasis and importance to Indian concept of Fine Arts. Especially, the scheme is not that helpful in respect of Indian Dance, Music, Theatre, Painting, Drama and Sculpture. There is no provision to individualise classics falling under Fine Arts as provided in CC, with the help of classic device. Works of individual artists can be individualised only by Alphabetical Device (AD) (e.g. 75 Rubens, Works of Rubens).

In respect of detailed schedule of Fine Arts, UDC has an edge over CC. The elaborate treatment of various branches of Fine Arts, well supported by several schedules of special auxiliary tables and common auxiliaries of various types will meet the requirements of those libraries specialised in Fine Arts. The notational techniques and various signs have enhanced the capacity of UDC for depth classification and transformed it into Faceted Scheme for Classification.

ANNEXURE-1 (UDC, IME, 1985)

70. The Arts, Recreation, Entertainment, Sport.

71. Physical Planning; Regional, Town and Country Planning; Landscapes, Parks, Gardens.

    711. Principles and Practice of Physical Planning.

    712. Planning of Landscape.

    718. Cemeteries, Graveyards, etc.

72. Architecture.

    721. Buildings Generally.

    725. Public, Civil, Commercial, Industrial Buildings.

    726. Religious, Ecclesiastical Architecture.

    727. Buildings for Education, Scientific, Cultural purposes.

    728. Domestic Architecture, Housing, Residential Buildings.

73. Plastic Arts, Sculpture, Numismatics, Metal Arts.

    730. Sculpture in General.

    736. Glyptics, Sigillography.

    737. Numismatics

    738. Ceramic Arts, Pottery.

    739. Metal Arts.

74. Drawing, Design, Applied Arts and Crafts.

    741. Drawing in General.

    742. Perspectives in Drawing.

    743. Anatomical Drawing.

    744. Linear Drawing.

    745. Decorative Handicrafts.

    746. Fancy works, Art Needlework.

    747. Interior Decoration.

    748. Vitreous Arts, Artistic Glass and Crystalware.

    749. Artistic furniture.

75. Painting (No further classification).
76. Graphic Arts, Graphics.
    761. Relief Techniques.
    762. Intaglio Techniques.
    763. Planographic Techniques.
    769. Collections of Graphics. Prints.
77. Photography and Similar Processes.
    771. Photographic Equipment.
    772. Photographic Systems (Using Inorganic substances).
    773. Photographic Systems (Using organic substances).
    774. Photomechanical Processes.
    776. Photolithography.
    777. Inlaglio and Relief Processes.
    778. Special Applications &Techniques.
    779. Collections of Photographs.
78. Music.
    781. Theories of Music.
    782. Dramatic Music.
    783. Church Music.
    784. Vocal Music.
    785. Instrumental Music.
    786. Music for Keyboard Instruments.
    787. Music for String Instruments.
    788. Music for Wind Instruments.
    789. Music for Percussion Instruments.
79. Recreation, Entertainment, Games, Sport.
    791. Public Entertainments.
    792. Theatre, Stage Craft, Dramatic Performances.
    793. Social Entertainments and Recreations.

794. Board and Table games.

796. Sport, Games, Physical Exercises.

797. Waterspouts, Aerial sports.

798. Riding and Driving, Animal Sports.

799. Fishing, Hunting, Shooting.

ANNEXURE-2

COLON CLASSIFICATION:
6th Edition (1960) and 7th Edition (1987) and UDC (1985) (Schedule of Basic Subjects in Fine Arts)

7th edn		6th edn	UDC (IME) (1985)
N	Fine Arts	N	7
.Nn	Ornament	?	?
Ns	Lapiday Art	NE	736.2
.Nt	Beedwork		746.5
Nv	Numismatic Art	NF	737
N1	Graphic Art	NM ..	76
.N3	Calligraphic Art		?
N5	Drawing	NP	741/744
N6	Painting	NQ	75
N7	Engraving (Graphic Art)	NN	762
.N8	Etching		762
.N91	Needlework		746
N93	Embroidary	NL	746.3
.N95	Lacework		746.2
.N97	Tapestry		745.52 and 645.23
NA	Architecture	NA	72
.NAT	Interior Decoration		747
.NAX	Furniture Design		684.4 and 794.1
NB	Town Planning	NB	711.4
NC	Plastic Art	NC ..	73
ND	Sculpture	ND	73/730
.NF	Artistic Glass	..	748
NH	Ceramic Art	NH	738
NJ	Inlay Art	NJ	674.24 & 684.6
.NL	Mosaic Art		738.5
NR	Music	NR	78
.NRV	Musical Instrument ..		681.8

NS	Dance	NS	793.3
NT	Theatre	NT	792
NU	Puppet Play	NU	791.5
NV	Shadow Play	NV	?
NW	Photography	NW(Cinema) 77	
NX	Cinematography	NX(Talkie) 778.5	

Note : CC (6th Edn) includes NG Mould Art and NK Toy-making under N Fine Arts. These two are not found in the 7th Edn. of CC.

REFERENCES

1. The Encyclopaedia Americana International Edition, Danbury, Connecticut; Giolier Inc., 1984 vol. 14, p. 555.
2. The New Encyclopaedia Britannica (Macropedia), vol. 2, 15th edn. Chicago: Encyclopaedia Britannica Inc., 1974, p. 81.
3. The Encyclopaedia of Arts, London: Thomas & Hudson, 1966, p. 229.
4. Dictionary of Arts, ed. by M.L. Wolf. New York: Philosophical Library, 1951, p. 271.
5. The New Encyclopaedia Britannica, (Micropedia), vol. 4, 15th edn. p. 140.
6. Andhra Vijnana Sarvaswamu, vol. 14, Hyderabad: Telugu Bhasa Samithi, 1979, p. 18.
7. Langridge, D.W., Classification and Indexing in the Humanities, London: Butterworths, 1976, pp. 78-94.
8. Ranganathan, S.R., Colon Classification, 7th edn. Bangalore : Sarada Ranganathan Endowment for Library Science, 1987, p. 43.
9. Ibid. p. 46.
10. Universal Decimal Classification (IME), Part I, London : British Standards Institution, 1985, p. ix.

6

Indology : Problems in its Classification and Organisation in Libraries with Special Reference to Universal Decimal Classification (IME, 1985) and Colon Classification 7th Edition, 1987)

DEFINITION AND SCOPE OF INDOLOGY

It is rather difficult to find a comprehensive and acceptable definition of Indology. The Oxford English Dictionary defined it as "the study of Indian history, literature, philosophy, etc." (7, p.227). The Websters New International Dictionary defined it as "the study of language, literature, history, philosophy, customs, etc. of India" (14, p. 1269). These definitions, of course, are not comprehensive as they fail to include some of the most important branches of Indology. Even the scholars of Indological studies both Indian and foreign have offered varied definitions and many of them are not comprehensive enough to include various branches of Indology. For the purpose of this paper it may be stated that

Indology is the study of History, Philosophy, Religion, Culture, Language, Literature (especially Sanskrit, Pali, Prakrit), Geography, Architecture, Epigraphy, Numismatics, Arts and Social life in ancient India. In essence it is the study of ancient Indian culture.

LIBRARY COLLECTIONS ON INDOLOGY

Most of the 180 Universities and University level Institutions in India possess varied and rich collections on Indological studies. Many of these Universities have Departments of Indology/Ancient Indian History, Culture and Archaeology, which offer courses at post-graduate level and carry out research and publication activity on various branches of Indology. The phenomenal development of indological studies in India and elsewhere resulted in mushroom growth of literature on Indology and posed challenge to the Librarians in India and abroad to classify the documents emanating from various branches of Indology (13).

Majority of the University libraries and Research Institutions in India follow Dewey Decimal Classification (various editions) and Universal Decimal Classification respectively for classification and organisation of their collections. Few Universities follow Colon Classification. The provision of schedules for various branches of Indology in the three Universal schemes — DDC, UDC and CC is not that satisfactory.

EXPANSION AND MODIFICATION OF SCHEDULES IN THE UNIVERSAL SCHEMES

In order to meet the needs of academic and special libraries in India and to give better treatment to various brunches of Indology, attempt have been made in i he past by the Indian Librarians to expand and modify especially the schedules of DDC. Balkrishan expanded the DDC schedule on Indian Philosophy for the benefit of libraries using DDC (I). S.K. Mookerjee had prepared a depth schedule entitled "Dewey Decimal expansion for Indic Subjects" (6). P.K. Banarjee prepared depth schedule of DDC for Indian philosophy which covers various branches and sub-branches (3). Pandey S.K, Sharma in his thesis, entitled "Expansion and modification of Dewey Decimal Classification for classifying. indological books" attempted to provide phoenix schedule for Indian Philosophy and religion for the aid of librarians and bibliographers dealing Indological books (12).

TREATMENT OF INDOLOGY IN THE UNIVERSAL SCHEMES

The treatment of Indology in the three universal schemes — DDC, UDC and *CC* differ widely. The DDC is the most popular scheme used by the Public and Academic Libraries in India. The "Report on the Development of Information and Library Network" stated that about 65 per cent of University libraries seem to follow Dewey Decimal Classification (4, p.64). But it is common knowledge that DDC has not given due treatment to various branches of Indology in its schedules. It has not come up to meet the growing needs of especially the academic libraries in India. The UDC which is based on the structure of DDC has inherited the lacunae in respect or treatment of Indology. The CC being the national scheme dealt various branches of Indology and its schedules are more hospitable to classify books on Indology. The pan *3* of CC deals schedules of classics and sacred books with special names. (ID). In the following sub-sections an attempt has been made to present the treatment of important branches of Indology in UDC (IME 1985) and CC (7th Edn. 1987).

INDIAN PHILOSOPHY

The output of literature of Indian Philosophical systems is enormous. Most of Academic and Public libraries in India possess rich and valuable collections on various branches of Indian Philosophy. These collections require proper classification and organisation to meet the ever growing demands of user community. The treatment of various branches of Indian philosophy in the schedules of UDC and CC is shown in Annexure I. There is no provision for Indian Philosophy in the schedule of UDC leave about its branches. The CC (7th Edn) lists various branches of Indian Philosophy under chapter DE - Schedule of Basic subjects. The Editor of 7th Edition of CC in his preface stated that "details of schedules have been developed and expanded wherever necessary and found essential. The expansion is such that it can be used in the sixth edition as well as in the seventh edition" (5). This perhaps means that the detailed schedule for Indian Philosophy in the 6th Edition holds good for 7th Edition also.

INDIC RELIGIONS

The schedule for Indic religions and their branches in the UDC is not satisfactory. The various aspects of Indic religion such as practices, sacred books, prayers, scriptures, cults, doctrines, festivals, gods and goddesses etc. have not found place in the UDC. However, CC has given better treatment to various aspects of Indian religions. In Annexure 2, important branches of Indic religions and their treatment in the schedules id UDC and *CC* is shown.

INDIAN HISTORY

Indian history dates back to 3000 years B.C. Great empires rose and fell in the Indian sub-content. Enormous literature has been published on various aspects and phases of Indian history. The political developments through centuries bad their impact on religion, art, language and literature (2, p.45). Academic Libraries in India possess very voluminous, rich and valuable collections on various facets of history of Indian sub-continent. Both UDC and CC have failed to provide a detailed schedule to classify the historical periods, dynasties, rulers of Indian history. Hut in CC with the help of chronological device, various periods of Indian history can be classified. In Annexure 3, important periods of Indian history up to the Pre-Muslim period has been given indicating their treatment in UDC and CC.

SANSKRIT LANGUAGE AND LITERATURE

Sanskrit is the mother of Indian languages and literatures. Most of the Hindu religious, philosophical, mystical medical and art works are in Sanskrit. Sanskrit had its impact on the development of other Indian languages and literatures. Not only Indian, but also British, German and French indologists have devoted their entire lives to give comprehensive account of the history of Sanskrit language and literature (9). The University and Oriental Research Institute Libraries in India possess enormous book collections on various facets of Sanskrit language and literature (8). There is no provision in the UDC to classify various aspects of Sanskrit including individual works of eminent poets, dramatists, novelists, critics and the like. The Parr *3* of CC (6th Lulu.) helps us to classify various aspects of Sanskrit literature in Annexure-4, important aspects of Sanskrit literature including few eminent authors is listed to show their provision or otherwise in the schedules of UDC and CC.

OTHER BRANCHES OF INDOLOGY

The other branches of Indology — Arts, Archaeology, Epigraphy, Geography, Numismatics, Social and Cultural life needs better appreciation and treatment by the; Universal classification schemes. Because of space constraint the treatment of these branches in the UDC and CC have not been dealt. But the discussion in the proceeding sections and the examples in the annexure clearly indicate that UDC has not given due consideration to Indology in its schedules.

LAW OF LOCAL VARIATION

To meet the requirements of a particular geographical area and to develop special collections, Ranganathan expounded the law of local variation which effects the notational plane of the scheme (II, p. 129). The said principle may he given due consideration by the editorial policy committee of UDC so as to meet the special requirements of countries and communities, concerned with Indology. UDC may think of developing special depth schedules on various branches of Indology to meet the requirements of libraries and information centres. This will go a long way in minimising the 'Western bias' to certain extent and transform it truly a Universal Scheme.

CC has an edge over UDC as for the treatment of Indology is concerned. This is demonstrated in the main schedules as well as Part 3 of CC. But Part 3 also requires revision and extension to include various languages and literatures of India, fine arts, performing arts, archaeology and numismatics. The revised schedule for these branches should be appended to the 7th Edn. of CC.

CONCLUSION

The usage of Universal Schemes especially the DDC and UDC is steadily increasing in the libraries of Indian sub continent. Therefore UDC must make a beginning for the provision of depth schedules for at least some *of* the important branches of Indology stated in sections 3.1.-3.1. The over emphasis for Sciences and Technologies in the UDC can be neutralised to certain extent by strengthening and expanding the schedules for Arts and Humanities with special reference to Indology. This policy will go a long way in minimising the problems of classification and organisation of documents of Indology in the libraries using UDC.

REFERENCES

1. Balkrishan. Indian Philosophy - Expansion. Indian Librarian 17 (1963), p 202-209.
2. Basham, A.L.: The wonder that was India, 3rd Rev. Edn. (Reprint), London, Sidwick & Jackson, 1982. 568 p.
3. Benerjee, P.K.: Some stray thoughts on Dewey Decimal Classification. Indian Librarian 27 (1972) No. 1, p. 12-18.
4. Development of Information and Library Networks, Report of Inter-Agency Working Croup. New Delhi, UGC, 1988. 173p.
5. Gopinath, M.A., Ed. Colon Classification. Edn. 7. Bangalore, Sarada Ranganathan Endowment for Library Science, 1987, 332p.
6. Mookerjee, S.K.: Development of Libraries and Library Science in India, Culcutta, World Press, 1969, Appendix C. p. 170-503.
7. The Oxford English Dictionary, Vol. V. Oxford. The Clarendon Press, 1961.
8. Raghavan, V.: Indological Studies in India, Delhi, Motilal Banarasidas, 1964, 35p.
9. Raghavan, V.: Sanskrit and Allied Indological studies in Europe, Madras

University of Madras, 1956, 117p.

10. Ranganathan, S.R.: Colon Classification, 6th Edn., Bombay, Asia Publishing House, 1969, Part 3, 3.3 3.126 p.
11. Ranganathan, S.R. Prolegomena to Library Classification, Edn. 3, Bombay, Asia Publishing House, 1967, 640 p.
12. Sharma, Pandey S.K. Expansion and modification of Dewey Decimal Classification for classifying Indological books, Ph.D. thesis approved by Punjab University, Chandigarh in 1977, 473p.
13. Sharma, Pandey, S.K.: Universe of Knowledge and Research Methodology, Delhi, Ken Publications, 1990, 473 p.
14. Websters New International Dictionary, Second Edn. Abridged, Springfield, G & C Merriam, 1954.

ANNEXURE 1 :
MAIN BRANCHES OF INDIAN PHILOSOPHY

	UDC*	CC
Hindu Philosophy	-	R61
Vaisesika	-	R621
Nyaya	-	R625
Sankhya	-	R631
Yoga	-	R635
Purva mimamsa	-	R64
Bhatta mimamsa	-	R641
Prabhakara mimamsa	-	R645
Vedanta	-	R65
Advaita	-	R66
Pratyabhijna	-	R663
Virasaivaadvaita	-	R6634
Visistadvaita	-	R67
Vaisnava	-	R672
Saiva Siddhanta	-	R673
Dvaita	-	R68
Bhedabheda	-	R6891
Davantadvaita	-	R6892
Sudhadvaita	-	R6893
Carvaka	-	R691
Jaina	-	R693
Budhistic	-	R694
Hinayana	-	R6941
Vaibhasika	-	R6942
Sautantrika	-	R6943
Mahayana	-	R6945
Yoga Cara	-	R6946
Madhyamika	-	R6947

* **Note:** UDC is completely silent about Indian Philosophy.

ANNEXURE 2:
MAIN BRANCHES OF INDIC RELIGIONS

	UDC	CC
Hinduism (Vedic)	293	Q,1
Rigveda	294.118	Q,11
Yajurveda	294.118	Q,12
Taithriya	-	Q,125
Vajasuneya	-	Q, 126
Madhyandina	-	Q,127
Samaveda	294.118	Q, 13
Talavakara	-	Q, 132
Ranayania	-	Q,133
Atharava Veda	294.118	Q,14
Saunakiya	-	Q.141
Hinduism (post-Vedic)	294.5	Q,2
Manu	-	-
Yajnavalkya	-	-
Smartaism	-	Q,21
Vaisnavism	294.512.14	Q,22
Pancarata	-	Q, 222
Saivism	294.512.14	Q,23
Agamic Saivism	-	Q,232
Kashmir Saivism	-	Q,233
Vira Saivism	-	Q,234
Ganapatysim	-	Q,24
Saktaism	-	Q,25
Sanmukaism	-	Q,26
Saurasim	-	Q,27
Jainism	294.35	Q,3
Svetambara	-	Q,31

Anga	-	Q,31;211
Upangas	-	Q,31;212
Prakirna	-	Q,31;213
Cheda-sutra	-	Q,31;214
Nandi and Anuyogadvara	-	Q,31;215
Mula-sutra	-	Q,31;216
Digambara	-	Q,32
Budhism	294.3 Q,4	
Hinayana	-	Q,41
Tripitaka	-	Q,41;2
Vinayapitaka	-	Q,41;21
Suttapitaka	-	Q,41;22
Abhidammapitaka	-	Q,41;23
Mahayana	-	Q,42
Lamaism	-	Q,43

ANNEXURE-3: IMPORTANT PERIOD DIVISIONS OF INDIAN HISTORY (PRE-MUSLIM INDIA)

	UDC	CC
Pre-historic period	934•	V,44'B
B.C. C. 3000 Agricultural Communities in Baluchistan		
C. 500 - 1500 The Harappa Culture		
Pre-Historic (Vedic) Period		
C. 1500-900 Composition of the Hymnes of the Rigveda		
C. 900 The Mahabharata War		
C. 900-500 Period of later Vedas, Brahmanas and early Upanishads		
Buddist Period C. 563-325		
Mauryan Period C. 322-163		
The Age of Invasions C. 190-71		
Satavahana Dynasty in deccan C. 50 BC - AD 250		
Gupta Period A.D. 320 - 647		
Madieval Dynasties of Northern India AD 712-1192	954, 02••	V,44'F92-D712
Medieval Dynasties of the Peninsula AD 300-1565		
300-888 Pallavas of Kanchi		
550-757 Chalukya Dynasty		
550- 790 Eastern Chalukyas of Vengi		
757-973 Rasthrakutas of Manyakheta		
850-1267 Cholas of Tanjore		
1110-1327 Hoyasalas of Dorasanudra		
1190-1294 Yadavas of Devagiri		
1197-1323 Kakatiyas of Warangal		
1216-1327 Pandyas of Madurai		
1336-1565 Vijayanagara Empire		

• History of Ancient India (to 647 AD)

•• History of Indian Sub-continent, 647-1774

Note: 1 . In UDC, with the help of Common Auxiliaries of Time the above period divisions of Indian History can be represented in the Class number.

2. In CC, with the help of Time Isolates the above period divisions can be

represented in the Class number.

ANNEXURE 4: SANSKRIT LITERATURE

	UDC	CC
Vedic Literature	891.2	0, 15A
Brahmanas		
Upanishads		
Epic Literature	891.2-13	0,15,1
Ramayana		0,15,A1
Mahabharata		0,15,A2
Poetry (Kayva)	891.2-1	0,15,1
Narrative Poetry		
Asvaghosa		
Kalidasa		
Megha		
Kashemendra		
Sriharsha		
Historical Poetry		
Bane		
Bilhana		
Kalhara		
Jahlana		
Hemachandra		
Emotional poetry		
Amaru		
Bhartrihari		
Jayadeva		
Mayura		
Devotional Poetry		
Mayura		
Harshavardhana		
Sankara		
Puspadanta		

Philosophical Poetry		
Nagarjuna		
Santideva		
Bimalachandra		
Gunobhadra		
Bhartrihari		
Drama (Nataka)	891.2-2	0,15,2
Asvaghosa		
Bhasa		
Kalidasa		
Sudraka		
Visakhadatta		
Harsa		
Fiction (Upanyasa)	891.2-3	0,15,3
Avadana		
Budhist Fiction		
Dharmakatha		
Champu		
Kathanaka		
Instructive tales		
Hitopedesa		
Katha		
Kathasarisagara		
Vratakatha		
Literary Criticism	891.2.09	D,15,g

Note. In CC, with the help of Classic Device, works of individual authors can be represented in the Class number.

Facet 3
LIS CURRICULUM

7

The Chequered History of LIS Curriculum

INTRODUCTION

Library and Information Science (LIS) education in India has gone a long way since the introduction of the first one year P.G. Diploma course at University of Madras in 1937 by S. R. Ranganathan. This course served almost as a model for the development of Library Science Programmes in the Country during the pre and post independent periods until 1950s. It has been estimated that there were five Universities conducting the Diploma Courses before independence. During the seventies the number rose to 42 and at present nearly hundred LIS Departments in the Universities, Colleges and Institutions have been offering Courses at different levels i.e. DLISc. MLISc, MLISc (Two Year Programme), M. Phil and Ph.D. There is no uniformity with regards to Course contents or the syllabi of these programmes. The syllabi of these courses were designed to meet the local requirements. Other facts that have had a bearing on the curriculum were the infrastructure facilities, strength of teaching staff and financial support from the parent organisations. After independence and specifically from 1960s and onwards, most of the LIS Departments formulated their syllabi keeping in view the syllabi formulated by the Review Committee appointed by the University Grants Commission in 1965 and headed by S. R. Ranganathan.[1]

MAJOR RECOMMENDATIONS OF THE REVIEW COMMITTEE

The Review Committee in its report traced the then existing facilities of teaching and research, and suggested syllabi for CLSc, BLISc, MLISc Programmes and identified sectors for research in Library Science and also made far reaching recommendations covering such aspects as: minimum qualifications for admission to courses, pre-admission course, university courses such as Ph.D., M.Lib.Sc. and B.Lib.Sc, methods of teaching and relative place of theory and practice, equivalence of Diploma in Library Science and B.Lib.Sc., non-professional subjects in the US Curriculum, examination, working hours, minimum qualifications for teachers, staff requirement, physical facilities, books, training of teachers, research, survey of trained personnel-needs and quality and cooperation between the Departments of Library Science and the Library.

Even after nearly four decades, many of the recommendations of the Committee remained only on Paper and many of the LISc Departments were not able to implement them thereby producing sub-standard products to manage libraries and Information Centres.

SYLLABI SUGGESTED BY THE REVIEW COMMITTEE

After stating the objectives of each course, the Committee identified detailed course contents under each paper to be offered at B.Lib.Sc. and M.Lib.Sc. levels. The following is the scheme of paper recommended for B.Lib.Sc. Course: 1. Library Organisation, 2. Library administration, 3. Physical Bibliography and Book Selection, 4. Document Bibliography and Reference Service. 5. Library Classification (Theory), 6. Library Classification (Practice), 7. Library Catalogue (Theory), 8. Library Catalogue (Practice) and 9. Record and Practical works.

The following is the scheme of Papers recommended for M.Lib.Sc. Course.

1. Universe of Knowledge; its development and structure.
2. Depth Classification (Theory)
3. Depth Classification (Practice)
4. Advanced Library Catalogue,
5. Any one of the following:
   a) Public Library System
   b) Academic Library System
   c) Research and Technical Library System,
   d) Documentation.
6. Project during term time, and
7. Literature Survey in any one of the fields such as:
   a) Indology
   b) Humanities
   c) Social Sciences
   d) Pure Sciences
   e) Applied Sciences
   f) Government documents and
   g) Juvenile literature

CHANGES IN BLISC CURRICULUM

For nearly two decades i.e. until 1980s most of the LIS Departments in the country to a greater extent followed the model syllabus recommended by the Review Committeewith certain modifications. After 1980s we could notice a marked change in the curriculum of BLISc/MLISc Programmes due to changes in the information scenario of the country and emerge of Information Science and Information technologies and slow adoption of information technologies in Libraries and Information Centres. The emphasis that was laid on physical and document bibliography in BLISc Course gave place to reference and Information Sources and Services: Library Organisation has been replaced by Library and Society (or Community). The emphasis on classification and cataloguing (Theory and Practice) has been reduced if not completely eliminated. Library Administration has been replaced by Library Management. In few Library Science Departments 'Computer Applications' has been included in BLISc Programme.

CHANGES IN MLISC CURRICULUM

The Masters Degree Programmes have undergone significant changes as a result of changes in the information scenario in the country. Most of the LIS Departments dropped the Paper on 'Universe of Knowledge' and reduced the over emphasis given to classification and cataloguing (Theory and Practice). The electives hither to occupied a prominent place in the curriculum have also been dropped. Some of the Departments even dropped project works and literature survey due to obvious reasons of usefulness and practicality (practicability). To a large extent the present MLISc Curriculum included such new areas as: Information and Communication, Information Systems and Programmes (or Services), Information Technology, Computer applications in Libraries, Resource sharing and Networking, Bibliographic databases and Networks and Research methods in LIS. The Review Committee has not given thought to M.Phil Programme, even thought it has made certain specific recommendations for Ph.D. Programmes.

UGC PANEL ON LIBRARY A INFORMATION SCIENCE

The UGC Panel on Library and Information Science at its meeting held on September 19, 1981, has formulated syllabi for BLISc/MLISc/M.Phil Programmes and in addition formulated guidelines with respect to: a) strength of the Faculty, b) qualification for teachers, e) Establishing/strengthening a Department.[2] The Panel also while appreciating the usefulness of (the then) existing pattern of Bachelor's and Master's degree courses in LIS at the P.G. levels, recognised the need for two year integrated programme in LIS. The recommendations of the LIS Panel were accepted by the UGC and circulated them to LIS

Departments in the country in January and March, 1982 for guidance and observation. The Panel identified the objectives of BLISc, MLISc, M.Phil and Ph.D. programmes and identified the following curriculum for each of these courses except Ph.D. Programme.

BLISc AND MLISc CURRICULUM

The Papers for BLISc include 1. Library and Society, 2. Library Classification (Theory), 3) Library Classification (Practice), 4. Library Cataloguing and Subject Indexing (Theory), 5. Library Cataloguing and Subject Indexing (Practice), 6. Reference and Information Sources, 7. Reference and Information Services and 8. Library Management and Administration. The Master's degree programme includes the following papers: 1. Universe of knowledge, 2. One of the following a) Information Storage and Retrieval, b) Depth Classification, 3. Information Systems and Programmes, A. Information and Literature Source in any one of the following: a) Humanities, b) Social Sciences, c) Sciences, d) Medical Sciences, d) Engineering and Technology, f) Agricultural Sciences, etc. 5. One of the following: a) Computer applications in Libraries/Information Centres, b) Comparative Librarianship, c) LIS Education; 6. Operations Research and systems analysis, 7. One of the following: a) Public Library System, b) Academic Library System, c) Research and Technical Library Systems, d) Agriculture Library Systems, e) Medical Library Systems, f) Engineering and Technological Library System and 8. Project and dissertation. The Curriculum for M.Phil Programme and consists of two parts. Art-I: consist three papers viz. 1. Research Methods, 2. Library Planning and Management and 3. Any of the following options: a) University and College library System, b) Research and Technical Library System, c) Public Library Systems, d) Information Processing and Organisation, e) Information transfer and dissemination, b) Comparative Librarianship and g) Education for LIS. Part-II: Dissertation. As regards Ph.D. programme the Panel recommendation states that "original research and theoretical and applied on any aspect of library and information science with a view to extending the knowledge boundaries of the discipline"[3].

INFLUENCE OF REVIEW COMMITTEE

The UGC Panel on Library and Information Science could not come out of the influence of the Review Committee as it has retained some of the papers suggested by the Review Committee even after nearly two decades. In BLISc Programme the emphasis given to classification and cataloguing (Theory and Practice) by the Review Committee has been retained by the UGC Panel. Library organisation and Library Administration (Papers 1 and 2) have been clubbed and re-designated as Library Management and Administration (Paper-8). Physical Bibliography and Document Bibliography (Papers 3 and 4) have been replaced by two papers: Reference and Information Sources and Services (Papers 6 and 7). The papers recommended for MLISc Programme by UGC Panel underwent few changes and modifications when compared with papers recommended by the Review Committee. The UGC Panel retained universe of knowledge (Paper-I). Depth Classification and Advanced Library Catalogue (Theory and practice) suggested by the Review Committee has been partially dropped by the UGC Panel contains Depth Classification as one of the electives under Paper-II. It includes two new Papers entitled Information Systems and Programmes (Paper-III) and Operations Research and Systems Analysis (Paper-VI). The Paper on Literature Survey (Paper-III) suggested by Review Committee has been retained in the syllabus suggested by UGC Panel as Paper-IV. The electives suggested by the Review Committee under Paper-V were retained by the UGC Panel under Paper-VII. The Project Report finds place in both models under Paper-VI (Review Committee) and Paper-VIII (UGC Panel). In addition, the UGC Panel included one more elective under Paper-V one of the following a) Computer applications, b) Comparative Librarianship and c) LIS Education. The two groups electives suggested by the UGC Panel for MLIS Course also find a place in the curriculum suggested for M.Phil Programme under Part-I, Paper-III. Any of the following options. It appears that different library systems such as Public, Academic, Special,

Research and Technical have greater influence and impact in the then contemporary LIS education in the country and therefore the framers of LIS Curriculum dared not to drop them even though the concept of different library systems have undergone radical changes and in the present Information scenario where the boundaries between different library systems have been fast vanishing after the advent of I.T. and emergence of sharing and Networking.

REPORT OF CDC ON LIS

The UGC in September 1990 appointed the Curriculum Development Committee (CDC) to restructure the courses of studies in LIS under the Chairmanship of Prof. P. N. Kaula. The Committee submitted its report and it was published by the UGC 1992/* The Committee identified the objectives of Courses such as BLISc, MLISc, MLISc (Integrated), M.Phil and Ph.D. The six core papers for BLISc include: 1. Library and Information Society, 2. Library and Information Management, 3. Library Classification (Theory and Practice), 4. Library Cataloguing and subject Indexing (Theory and Practice) 5. Information Sources and Services, and 6. Computer Applications. It has identified sixteen elective papers for BLISc Programme. The Curricula for MLISc (One Year Programme) consists of both core as well elective papers. The five core papers care 1. Information and Communication: Evolution and Development, 2. Library and Information Management, Sources and Services, 3. Computer Technology, Library Automation and Information System, 4. Information Processing and Retrieval and 5. Research Methodology and Informatics. The six elective Papers includes:

1. Comparative and International Librarianship.
2. Higher Education and Academic Library System,
3. Communication, Mass Media and Public Library,
4. Bibliographic control.
5. User education and user studies, and
6. Education for Library and Information Science.

MLISC TWO YEAR PROGRAMME

The MLISc (Two Year Programme) integrated course consists of five core papers for first year and four core papers for second year and also two groups of optional papers. Each group consists of ten papers of which a candidate shall have to opt for to electives in the previous year and two in the final year i.e. one each from groups A and B.

The first year core papers include

1. Foundations of Librarianship.
2. Library and information Management,
3. Library Classification (Theory and Practice)
4. Library Cataloguing and Indexing (Theory and Practice), and
5. Information Sources and Services.

The second year core papers include

1. Information and communication,
2. Information processing and Retrieval,
3. Computer applications and
4. Research Methodology and Informatics.

The Optional Papers under Group-A consists of

1. Higher education and Academic Library System,
2. Communication, Mass Media and Public Library System,
3. School and Children's Libraries,
4. Medical Libraries,
5. Law Libraries
6. Music libraries,
7. Engineering and Technology Libraries,
8. Agricultural Libraries,
9. Industrial Libraries, and
10. Archive Libraries.

The Optional Papers under Group-B Include

1. Bibliographic Control,
2. Education for LIS,
3. User studies and user education,
4. Comparative and International Librarianship,
5. Manuscroptology,
6. Preservation and conservation,
7. Learning skills and Reading Habits,
8. Library Buildings,
9. Local Studies Librarianship, and
10. Non-book materials.

M. Phil AND Ph.D. PROGRAMMES

The CDC Report suggested four papers for M.Phil Programme. These include

1. Research Methodology,
2. Current Trends in Library A Information Science,
3. Literature Survey, and
4. Dissertation and viva-voce.

The main objectives of this programme is to identify problem areas and appiy me hods of research to find solutions to problems, to formulate research proposals and to effectively present projects and / or dissertations.

The CDC Report also stated the objectives of Ph.D. programme and identified some of the areas related to LIS. The to objectives stated are 1. To undertake research work independently and 2. To give specialised knowledge in depth on any topic related to LIS, allied subjects and inter disciplinary areas. The broad areas identified for carrying out research are:

1. Structure and Development of knowledge,
2. Classification, Cataloguing and Indexing,
3. Informatric Studies in Library and allied subjects,

4. Computer Applications,
5. Historical Studies in Library and allied subjects,
6. Social and Economic aspects of Librarianship,
7. Library and Information Management and Systems analysis,
8. Application of techniques of library and information science to evaluate other disciplines.

REACTIONS AND COMMENTS ON CDC REPORT

There had been adverse reactions and comments on CDC Report. The teaching community by and large has not favorably reacted to the said report. The report failed to take into consideration ground realities obtaining in LIS Departments in the Country. There has been overlapping courses suggested for BLISc, MLISc and M.Lib.Sc. (Two Year) Programmes. The number of optionals / electives suggested for the said programmes is baffling and one wonders whether the required expertise and infrastructure was available in the LIS Departments. The Committee was 'choosy' in selecting the experts/resource persons which it has consulted and invited its "Own people" for participate in the workshop held on 12th February, 1991. In the opinion of critics the Committee failed to undertake critical review of the existing syllabi and courses of study at different levels and regions of the country and suggest appropriate and suitable measures for modernising the same and restructuring them to Unit Courses. The report failed to make LIS Education more meaningful and reflect the needs and aspirations of its beneficiaries as well as to make it more relevant to changing information scenario in the country. The list of books recommended at the end of each course is awfully presented with overlaps and bibliographical errors. It appears that University of Delhi has brought out revised CDC Report.

UNESCO (PGI) MODULAR CURRICULUM

UNESCO (PGI) has issued "A Modular Curriculum in Information Studies", prepared by J. A. Large in 1987 for the benefit of the member States[5]. This is intended as a resource from which curricula can be constructed by individual LIS Schools to meet the local needs and requirements. The said document lists twelve core modules as well as eight elective modules. The titles of core modules include 1. Information in its social and communication context, 2) Information Users, 3. Quantitative methods, 4. Research methods, 5. Information Sources, 6. Information storage and retrieval systems, 7. Information services, 8. Electronic data processing, 9. Application of information technology, 10. Telecommunications and networking in information systems, 11. Management of information systems and services, and 12. Economics and marketing of information. The titles of elective modules include 1. Design of Computer assisted information systems, 2. Sectoral / subject oriented information sources and systems, 3. Planning and design of buildings and facilities for information centres and libraries, 4. Online searching, 5. Health and welfare library and information services, 6. Agricultural library and information services. 7. Audio-visual studies, 8. Printing, book binding and conservation. The said document also provides for titles of other possible elective modules at Page 74.

IMPACT OF MODULAR CURRICULUM

The modular curriculum has some impact on LIS Departments in the Universities. Many of the Departments have included some of the modules with modifications in their syllabus especially for Master's Degree Programmes. This document reflects to certain extent the needs of LIS Schools in developing countries.

Some of the modules listed in the UNESCO document find a place in the CDC Report with some modifications.

UGCS FRESH INITIATIVE

The CDC Report was not given enough thought and chance for its implementation if not in toto, but partially, by the US Departments in the country. Fresh initiative was taken by the UGC Panel on Library and Information Science to discuss the report of

CDC and its implementation. In fact the earlier Panels on Library and. Information Science constituted by the UGC have critically looked into the CDC report and offered comments for its implementation. Perhaps, the said comments either were not brought to the notice of the present Panel on LIS by the concerned authority or the present Panel ignored those comments with a view to give fresh thought on it. Within the elapse of six years after the submission of CDC Report and without giving a chance for its implementation, a new exercise has been thought of by convening zonal meetings consisting of Chairpersons of Boards of Studies in LIS of the Universities and other Institutions "to discuss the report of CDC and its implementation". Already three zonal meetings were held at Kurukshetra (North), Bhubaneshwar (Central) and Hyderabad (South).

The said zonal meetings appeared to be closed door meetings confined only to Chairpersons of BOS in LIS and few of LIS Panel Members. The Heads of Departments were not officially invited. Even the senior faculty members and other experts available locally, were not invited.

It is rather surprising, may difficult to understand this 'touch me not' policy on the part of those who convened the zonal meetings. Let us hope that the four zonal committee meetings will help to bringing out a transformed CDC Report for its implementation or bring out a completely new report on LIS curriculum for the benefit of the LIS Departments in the Country.

CONCLUSION

Mere drawing up wonderful curriculum in LIS is not the end of the matter. The beginning of the matter is the capacity of the individual LIS Departments in the country for implementation. The present scenario of staff strength, infrastructure facilities like building, computer lab, library facilities, and other related aspects must be given due thought and make suitable recommendations to the UGC for its implementation. Unless the UGC comes in a big way to strengthen LIS Departments in respect of staff and infrastructure and other facilities mere revamping up of CDC Report or drawing up of completely 'new' curriculum in LIS, keeping in view the present IT scenario in the country may not serve the purpose. Let us wait for what is in store for LIS education in the country for the next century.

REFERENCES

1. *Library Science in Indian Universities*, Report of the UGC Review Committee, New Delhi, UGC, 1965.
2. *Recommendations of the Panel on Library and Information Science*, New Delhi, UGC, 1982.
3. Ibid, p. 3.
4. *Report of the Curriculum Development Committee on Library and Information Science*, New Delhi, UGC, 1992.
5. Large, J.A. *A Modular Curriculum in Information Studies*, Peris, UNESCO, 1987.

8

A Study of Marketing Component in MLISc Courses in India

INTRODUCTION

Library and Information Science Education in the Country at the Master's Degree level has gone a long way since the introduction of MLISc Programme, for the first time in the entire Commonwealth of Nations, at the University of Delhi in 1948. As per the UGC Curriculum Development Committee (CDC) Report (2001) on Library and Information Science, almost 145 LIS Schools have been offering Masters' Degree Programmes[1]. Unlike in 1970's most of LIS Schools have followed the model syllabus suggested by UGC Review Committee headed by Dr. S. R. Ranganathan with minor modifications[2]. There is no trace of *'marketing'* component in this model syllabus. In the year 1982, the UGC Panel on LIS has circulated a model syllabus for both BLIS / MLIS Programmes[3]. In the syllabus for MLIS programe there was no mention of 'marketing concept'. The Curriculum Development Committee (CDC) on LIS appointed by the UGC in its report published in 1992 has strangely offered a course on ***'Marketing of Information'*** under special courses but not in the core papers of MLISc Programme[4].

The UGC Model Curriculum for Library and Information Science (Karisiddappa Committee on Curriculum Development in LIS) in Module-3: Information Sources, Products and Services listed "Information Products: Nature, Concept, types, Design, Development and *Marketing* under Unit-IV: Information Services and Products[5]. But in the model syllabus for Master's Degree Programme (2 year Integrated Course) there is no specific mention of 'marketing' in any of the XV Papers listed for the said programme. It can be inferred that under Paper-IX: Information and Communication (2 years MLISC Integrated Programme) the topic 'Economics of Information' was listed under Unit-4. But there is no further elaboration of this topic to include 'marketing'.

The Modular Curriculum for higher degree programmes in Information Studies specially meant for developing countries prepared and circulated by General Information Programme (PGI) of UNESCO under core Module C-12 specified "Economics and Marketing of Information" with a detailed module content[6] (see Annexure-1). Another PGI (UNESCO) document titled *"Guidelines for teaching of marketing in the training of librarians, documentalists and archivists"* has identified six modules covering various facets of marketing of LIS Services and Products[7].

INCLUSION OF MARKETING CONCEPT IN LIS SYLLABI

The advent of teaching LIS at the university level especially in North America 'user survey methods', have been included in the course contents of number of higher learning institutions. Most of the research activity carried under this area aimed at obtaining a better knowledge of the users of library services. It was therefore, but natural that information specialists should develop an interest in the marketing of their services. The marketing concept was not really developed until after Second World War. It was not until 1969, that a famous American marketing expert Philip Kotler suggested the application of marketing concept to service organizations and non-profit making bodies[8].

Slowly and steadily LIS schools especially in North America

and European Continent have included 'marketing concept' in their syllabi. Indian LIS Schools have no exception in this regard. But the inclusion of marketing concept of LIS Syllabi has started in the 1990's. Now we may find that most of the LIS Schools in India have included 'marketing concept' in the syllabi of Master's Degree programmes with varying degree emphasis and nomenclature.

DEFINITION AND SCOPE OF MARKETING

There are several text-book definitions which define the concept of 'marketing' and identify its scope. Philip Kotler the renowned authority on marketing defines "marketing management the analysis, planning, implementation and control of carefully formulated programmes designed to bring about voluntary exchange of values with target markets for the purpose of achieving organizational objectives". In the context of marketing of LIS services and products, the scope includes: marketing approach as a management tool, marketing and behavior patterns, marketing research, marketing mix, supply and communication strategies and marketing strategy and planning[9].

In the light of the above scope of marketing of LIS services and products, the inclusion of these areas in the syllabi of MLIS programes of some of the Library Schools / Departments in Indian Universities is presented in the following paras.

STUDY OF UNIVERSITIES' SYLLABI

As Stated already the inclusion of marketing concept in the syllabi of the MLISc programes in the Universities in India started in the 1990's due to the influence of 'management studies' and programmes. It was also felt and recognized by the experts that information / knowledge is an important resource for national development. To harness it properly by applying marketing concepts was another important factor. Consequently the need for marketing of LIS services and products and the inclusion of this concept has been felt by LIS experts, teachers and practicing librarians. The curriculum Development Committees on LIS appointed by the UGC have recognized the need for and importance of inclusion of marketing concept in the syllabus of MLIS programme. The Curriculum Development of Committee (1992) appointed by UGC and headed by P.N. Kaula included 'marketing of information' as a special course. This is the beginning of inclusion of marketing concept in the syllabi of several universities in India offering MLIS Programmes.

The study is based on the syllabi of the LIS Departments of the following Universities and Institutions (Table-1) and may not give the clear picture of the present position of the inclusion of marketing concept as it is confined to only twelve universities.

Table 1: List of Universities / Institutions

S. No.	Name of the University / Institution	Abbreviation.	Syllabus for the year
1	Andhra University	AU	1994
2	Dr. B.R. Ambedkar Open University	BRAOU	1998
3	Gulbarga University	GU	1995
4	Indira Gandhi National Open University	IGNOU	1994
5	Indian National Scientific Documentation Centre	INSDOC	1995
6	Kakatiya University	KU	1993
7	Mangalore University	MU	?
8	Nagarjuna University	NU	1994
9	Osmania University	OU	1999
10	Sambalpur University	SU	1991
11	University of Calicut	UC	1996
12	University of Mysore	UM	?

The study revealed that there is no separate paper on 'Marketing of LIS Services and Products' in the syllabi of above universities except University of Mysore.

The topic has been listed under some paper or the other. The following Table-2 gives us an idea as to the listing of this concept under a particular paper.

Table 2 : Listing of Marketing Concept under a particular paper

S. No.	Name of the Uni.	Title of the Paper	S.No. of the Paper	Topic Nomenclature.
1	AU	Information Services	V	Marketing Information Service
2	BRAOU	Information Communication and Society	I	Marketing (Unit-13)
3	GU	Elements of Information Science	I (Final)	Marketing of Information (Unit-9)
4	IGNOU	Management of Information Centres	V	Marketing of Inf. Products and Services (Block 5, Unit-1)
5	INSDOC	Information Products and Services	VI	Marketing of Inf. Services and Products
6	KU	Information Science	IV	Marketing of Information
7	MU	Information Systems and Services	VI	Marketing of Information Services and Products
8	NU	Information Sources and Services	V	Marketing of Information
9	OU	Information and Communication	I	Marketing of Information Under Unit-4, Economics of Information
10	SU	Information Systems and Services	III	Marketing of Information Products and Services
11	UC	Information Systems and Services	VI	Marketing of Information Products and Services
12	UM	Economics and Marketing of Information	IV	Economics of Information; Market Analysis; Inf. Market Environment; Strategies for marketing of Inf. Products and services

An analysis of Table-2 reveals that there is no uniformity in the titles of the papers under which marketing concept has been listed. AU (1) listed the topic under Paper-V: Information Services. BRAOU (2) listed under Paper-I: Information, Communication and Society. GU (3) and KU (6) have listed under the papers Paper-I: Elements of Information Science and Paper-IV: Information Science respectively. Whereas IGNOU (4) has listed under Paper-V: Management of Information Centres. INSDOC (5) listed under Paper-VI: Information products and Services. Three universities viz. MU (7) (Paper-VI) SU (10) (Paper-III) and UC (11) (Paper-VI) have listed under the paper titled "Information Systems and Services". NU (8) has listed the topic under the Paper-V: Information Sources and Services, whereas OU (9) has listed under the Paper-I: Information and Communication.

University of Mysore (UM-12) has the distinction of having exclusively a separate paper on the topic. This University under Paper-IV: Economics and Marketing of Information listed various facets of marketing of library services and products.

TOPIC NOMENCLATURE

There is no uniformity in the syllabi of the twelve universities as to the topic nomenclature. These twelve universities have used different nomenclature such as: marketing information services (1); marketing (2), marketing of information (3, 6, 8, 9); marketing of information products and services (4, 5, 7, 10, 11); strategies for marketing of information products and services (12). Out of the twelve universities syllabi studied, five universities such as: IGNOU, INSDOC, Mangalore University, Sambalpur University and University of Calicut have used the nomenclature 'marketing of information products and services'. Four universities such as Gulbarga, Kakatiya, Nagarjuna and Osmania have used the nomenclature 'marketing of information'.

INFERENCES

The study revealed that the need for and importance of

inclusion of marketing concept in the syllabi of MLISc Programes offered by the Departments of LIS of Indian Universities. Except University of Mysore which offers of separate paper on "Economics and Marketing of Information", the remaining eleven Universities have just included a topic on 'marketing of library services and products'. This is a positive trend in the sense that the traditional areas / subjects have been slowly giving place to emerging subject fields such as marketing and information technologies. The study also revealed that emphasis on marketing differs from

University to University. It is left to the experts in the field to what extent emphasis should be laid and importance be given to marketing concept in the syllabi of MLIS Programmes in the context of all pervading information and communication technologies which have occupied a prime position in the LIS syllabi of Indian Universities. If one wish to give due place and importance to marketing concept in the syllabus of MLIS Programme the modules suggested in the *"Guidelines for teaching marketing in the training of librarians, documentalists and archivists"* requires due attention and consideration[10]. The module is provided in Annexure-2 for reference.

CONCLUSION

In order to teach 'marketing concept' to the students, of MLIS effectively and turn out quality products in this area from the portals of LIS Departments in the Country some of the faculty members of the Departments, if not all, require some training in the teaching of marketing concept. The topic has a great potential and teaching the topic both theoretical and practical as well will go a long way in turning out quality products who can meet the requirements of knowledge industries which are fast expanding in our country and elsewhere.

REFERENCES

1. *UGC Model Curriculum : Library and Information Science.* New Delhi, UGC, 2001. pp.123-145.

2. *Library Science in Indian Universities.* Report of the UGC Review Committee. New Delhi, UGC, 1965.

3. *UGC Panel on Library Science. Syllabus of LIS.* New Delhi, UGC, 1982. (Mimeographed).

4. *Report of the Curriculum Development Committee on Library and Information Science.* New Delhi, UGC, 1992. p. 108.

5. *UGC Model Curriculum. Library and Information Science.* Opcit. P. 21.

6. Large, J.A. A Modular Curriculum in Information Studies. Paris, UNESCO, 1987. p.56.

7. Savard, Rejean. Guidelines for the teaching of marketing in the training of librarians documentalists and archivists. Paris, UNESCO, 1988. p. 13-76.

8. Ibid. P.2.

9. Ibid, pp.35-76.

10. Ibid.

ANNEXURE-1:
C-12 ECONOMICS AND MARKETING OF INFORMATION MODULE CONTENT

Economics of Information

Economic analysis models and their application to the information industry; information as a commodity; information as a resource; trans-border data flows; barriers to information access - economic, political, legal, linguistic, cultural.

Market Analysis

Techniques and tools of market analysis - Collection of data, statistical analysis, forecasting, models of information markets; structure of domestic and external information markets; financial modeling.

Information Market Environment

Information markets in Europe, North American, South America, Asia and Australia; information marketing and new technologies; public and private sector markets; cultural attitudes and marketing.

Strategies for Marketing of Information Products

Planning; designing products and services to meet user needs; market segmentation; new product development; pricing policies; costing, internal and external factors affecting market behaviour; information use promotion - advertising; re-packaging of information products; value added process information production, transfer and use.

Source: Large, J. A. *A Modular Curriculum in Information Studies.* Paris, UNESCO, 1987. p. 56.

ANNEXURE-2
MARKETING COURSE CONTENT

Module1. Marketing Approach

1.1 Information service as a open system

1.2 What is marketing?

1.3 Development of marketing concept

1.4 The marketing mix

Module-2. Marketing and Behavior Pattern

2.1 Why information seeking behavior is important?

2.2 Pattern of Information seeking behavior

2.3 Key concepts for the study of information seeking behavior

Module-3. Marketing Research

3.1 Marketing Research

3.2 Preparation of Marketing Research

3.3 Types of Research

3.4 Sampling

3.5 After the data has been collected

Module-4. The Marketing mix - supply

4.1 Analysis of the supply

4.2 The product

4.3 Distribution

4.4 Staff

4.5 Price

Module-5. The Marketing mix - Communication Strategies

5.1 What is Marketing Communication?

5.2 The Planning of Advertising

5.3 Public Relations

5.4 Promotional Activities

Module-6. Marketing Strategy and Planning

6.1 Strategic Planning

6.2 Market Segmentation

6.3 The Target Public

6.4 The Marketing Plan

Source. *Savard, Rejean. Guidelines for the teaching of marketing in the training of librarians, documentalists and archivists.* Paris, UNESCO, 1988. pp.13-76.

9

A Study of IT Component in MLISc Cources in India

INTRODUCTION

Library and Information Science Education in the country at Masters' Degree level has gone a long way since the introduction of MLISc Degree for the first time by Dr.S.R.Ranganathan at the University of Delhi in 1948. At present nearly 50 University LIS Departments/Library Schools have been offering Masters' Degree programmes in LIS. Until 1970s most of the library schools have followed the model syllabus suggested by UGC Review Committee headed by Dr.S.R. Ranganathan with certain modifications. There is no trace of IT component in this syllabus. In the year 1982 the UGC Panel on Library & Information Science has circulated model syllabus for both BLISc/MLISc programmes. In the MLISc Syllabus prepared by the LIS Panel a paper on Computer Applications in Libraries/Information Centres was included as one of the electives under Paper-V. The Curriculum Development Committee (CDC) on LIS of UGC in its report published in 1992 has included under Paper-V: Computer Applications for BLISc Course. For Master's Degree Programme the CDC Report under Core papers for MLISc

(1 year programme) included a paper entitled Computer Technology, Library Automation and Information Systems (Paper-II), and for MLISc (2 Year Integrated Programme) in the second year under Paper—II: Computer Technology; Library Automation and Information Systems.

The modular curriculum for higher degree programmes in Information Studies especially meant for developing countries, prepared and circulated by General Information Programme (PGI) of UNESCO has under core modules included: Electronic Data Processing (C-08), and Telecommunications and Networking in Information Systems. (C-19).

NEED FOR IT COMPONENTS IN THE SYLLABI

The advent and development in Information Technology especially Computer, Communication, Document Processing and Delivery Technologies have been revolutionizing library and information services in developed countries . The Developing Countries have been slow in adopting IT in Libraries and Information Centres. But in the last one decade Library& Information Centres in India have been making concerted efforts for adopting IT to meet the varied information requirements and to be more resilient towards the demands of the user communities. In order to meet the demands for trained manpower in IT, LIS Departments have to update their syllabi incorporating various facets of IT. This will enable the library schools to sell their products in the market.

The thrust of this paper is to study and assess IT component in the syllabi of MLISc offered by LIS Departments/Institutions in the Country. The Syllabi of 15 LIS Departments/Institutions have been taken up for study.

DEFINITION AND SCOPE OF IT

It is rather difficult to offer or cite an acceptable and classic definition of IT. The scope and components of IT are also difficult to specify and identify. It differs from specialist to specialist in the field. Peter Zorkoczy cited two definitions which are as follows:

1. "Information Technology means the collection, storage processing, dissemination and use of information. It is not confined to hardware and software, but acknowledges the importance of man and the goals he sets for this technology, the values employed in making the choices, the assessment criteria used to decide whether he is controlling the technology and is being enriched by it".
2. "The scientific, technological and engineering disciplines and the management techniques used in information handling and processing; their applications; computers and their interaction with men and machines; and associated social, economic and cultural matters".

As regards scope and content of IT it has been suggested that it is an aggregation of several component technologies such as : Micro electronics, Optical electronics , Computer technology, Electronic office equipment, Telecommunications, Robotics, Artificial intelligence, Expert systems, Computer Controlled machines, Computer Input, Output and Storage devices and controlled systems . N Ravi the Editor of Hindu, identified three broad areas of IT viz. computers, communications and storage technologies.

STUDY OF UNIVERSITIES SYLLABI

The emerging IT scenario in the country has put in greater responsibilities on LIS Departments to include IT components in their syllabi so as to turn out the required manpower needed by Libraries and Information Centres some of which have already adopted IT or in the process of introducing IT in the operations and services. The syllabi of the LIS Departments of the following Universities and Institutions has been selected for study. The study based on the syllabi of 15 Universities listed in Table-1 may not give clear picture of the present situation.

Table 1. List of Universities/Institutes

Sl.No.	Name of the Univ/Inst.	Abbreviation	Syllabus for the year
1.	Andhra University	AU	1994
2.	Birla Institute of Technology	BIT	1994
3.	Gulbarga University	UG	1995
4.	Indira Gandhi National Open Univ.	IGNOU	1994
5.	Indian National Scientific and Documentation Centre	INSDOC	1995
6.	Karnataka University	KU	1993
7.	Nagarjuna University	NU	1994
8.	North Eastern Hill University	NEHU	1995
9.	Osmania University	OU	1996
10.	Sambalpur University	SU	1991
11.	Sri Venkateswara University	SVU	1996
12.	University of Calicut	UC	1996
13.	University of Delhi	UD	1993
14.	University of Madras	UM	1992
15.	Utkal University	UU	1996

NOMENCLATURE

The study reveals that (see Table-II) there is no uniformity with regards to nomenclature or title of papers covering IT components in the syllabi of the 15 universities listed in Table-II. Seven Universities/Institutions viz. BIT, GUS, INSDOC, KU, NU, NEHU and OU have split the field of IT into two courses/papers. For example BIT and INSDOC titled it as: IT (I): Computer Sciences & Technology and IT (II): Application/Networks. The other five Universities viz. GU, KU, NU, NEHU and OU titled it as 1. Information & Communication Technology/basics of Information and Communications Technology/Introduction to IT/Basics of IT and 2. Introduction to Computers/Computer Applications in Libraries/ Computer Applications in Library & Information Services. The remaining eight universities devoted either in one paper exclusively to Applications of IT/Introduction to IT/ Computer Applications in Libraries or mixing the two fields/areas in one course/paper. The nomenclature used by these Universities supports this view. For example AU and IGNOU titled it as: Application of IT, SU—IT, SVU & UM as: Introduction to IT, UC & UD as : Computer applications in Library and Information Services and UU as : IT and computer Application.

Except UD, the remaining 14 Universities have included IT and its components in one Course or two Courses under core papers. But UD put it under elective/optional paper. The syllabus of UD suffers from giving due importance and emphasis to IT. This is evident from Table II: Title of Papers (See Annexure-I).

TITLES OF PAPERS

An analysis of titles of papers offered by the 15 universities indicate that IT and Computer Applications form the core part. The titles of the papers are broadly fall into nine categories. Theses nine categories of titles and their commonness in more than one university is indicated in Table III: Analysis of Titles of Papers (See Annexure-II). An analysis of the titles of papers reveal that II and Computer applications in libraries are offered as two independent papers in most of the University except at Utkal University (15) where the two areas are clubbed into one paper i.e. IT and Computer Applications. The two papers viz. IT Part-I and Part-II (Sl.Nos.3, 4 and 5) are almost similar at BIT (2) and INSDOC (5). Like wise the two papers mentioned at Sl.Nos. 7 & 8 are common to GU (3) and KU (6).

The syllabi of 15 Universities have not clearly stated the practical component of IT and Computer Applications in Libraries. In most of the Universities, these two papers are offered as theory papers with little emphasis on practical. The BIT(2) in Paper IT (II); Application, provides practicals in Computer Languages and Software Packages. UD (13) mentions under paper VII (C):Computer Applications in Libraries "practical works and studies".

COURSE CONTENTS

It is rather difficult to divide the scope of IT into well defined and acceptable areas/components. Opinion differs from expert to expert and text-book to text-book on the subject. However for the purpose of studying the contents of the syllabi of 15 Universities on the subject, IT has been broadly divided into: 1) Communication Technology, 2) Computer Technology, 3) Reprography and Micrography and 4) Printing and Publishing Technology. These four areas are basic and core to IT. The coverage of these areas and their sub areas in the syllabi of 15 universities is presented in the Table -IV Analysis of Topics. (See Annexure III).

The study of the course contents of the 15 Universities reveal that there is a variance of coverage of topics which come under Communication Technology. The areas such as: Telecommunications, Communication Media, Networks/ Networking and Network Services have been covered by the syllabi of : BIT (2), Gu(3), IGNOU(4), INSDOC (5), KU (6), NU (7), NEHU (8), OU (9), SVU (11), UC (12), UM (14) and UU (15). In the syllabi of AU (1), SU (10), UD (13), these topics do not find a place.

The areas listed under Computer Technology viz. Hardware, Software, DBMS, Data Bases, Online Data Bases, Programming (Languages), Library Automation, Computer based Information Services, Artificial Intelligence, Data Processing and Information Retrieval find a place in the syllabi of almost all the 15 Universities. In addition to the above two major components of IT, areas such as; AV, Micrographic and Reprographic technology find place in the syllabi of GU (3), IGNOU (4), KU (6), NU (7), NEHU (8) and UC (12) and 2) Printing and Publishing Technology finds a place in IGNOU (4), UC (12), UM (14) and UU (15).

In the syllabus of SU (10) under Paper-V: Information Technology only two Units i.e. I and V deal with IT and Computer Technology. The rest of the units i.e. II - IV are devoted to Information Consolidation, Indexing and Abstracting.

The Syllabus of UC (12) under Paper - V: Computer Applications in Library & Information Services includes certain aspects of Communication, Micrographic technology and Search Strategy and Techniques.

INFERENCES

The study revealed that the impact of IT has been felt by the LIS Departments in the Country and it is evident that various aspects/areas of IT have been included in the syllabi of MLISc Programmes either in the form of one paper or two papers. This is a positive trend in the sense that the traditional areas of LIS have been slowly giving place to the emerging information technologies. As stated already emphasis has to be laid on practical training in IT. The study revealed that there is no coherence and logical structuring of various aspects of IT listed under broad areas viz. Communication, Computer, Micrographic and Printing and Publishing Technologies. The syllabus provided for IT in the CDC Report of UGC needs to be revised and improved. Whether this National Seminar can draft a model syllabus on IT?

CONCLUSION

In order to teach the various aspects of IT very effectively and turn out quality products from the portals of LIS Departments in the country the Faculty Members of the Departments if not all, at least some of them require education and training in IT and related technologies. To impart quality education and training to the students of LIS, the Departments of LIS in the Country should be strengthened with proper infrastructure facilities. The UGC should extent necessary financial support during the IX Plan Period to the Departments of LIS.

REFERENCES

1. Library Science in Indian Universities: Report of the UGC Review Committee, New Delhi, UGC, 1965.
2. UGC Panel on Library & Information Science. Syllabi of LIS New Delhi, UGC, 1982 (Mimeographed).

3. Report of the Curriculum Development Committee on Library & Information Science. New Delhi, UGC, 1992.

4. Large, J.A. A modular curriculum in Information Studies. Paris, UNESCO, 1987.

5. Gopinath, M.A. Information Technology, Knowledge processing and Libraries of the future; an integrated information service (In Information access through Networks; working papers for CALIBER 1995). Hyderabad. University of Hyderabad, 1995. P 129.

6. Zorkoczy, Peter and Heap, Nicholas. Information Technology, an introduction. 4th Ed. London, Pitman Publishing, 1995. P11 .

7. Gopinath, M.A. Op.cit. P 130.

8. Ravi, N, Ed. Preface (In The Hindu speaks on Information Technology). Madras, Kasturi & Sons, 1993. P.III.

ANNEXURE I

Table 2. Titles of Papers

Sl. No.	Name of the Uni.	Title of the Paper	Sl.No. of the Paper	Core/ Elective	Sem. (SM) Non-Sem.	One Year/ Two
1.	AU	Application of IT.	VI	Core	NSM	Two Years (Pr)
2.	BIT	1. IT (I): Computer Science and Technology.	II	Core	SM(1)	Two Years
		2. IT (II): Applications.	II	Core	SM (3)	Two Years
3.	GU	1. Introduction to Computers	VI	Core	NSM	Two Years (Pr)
		2. Information and Communication Technologies.	IV	Core	—	Two Years (Fin)
4.	IGNOU	Application of IT	VI	Core	NSM	One Year
5.	INSDOC	1. IT Part-I: Computer Science and Technology	V	Core	SM (1)	Two Years
		2. IT Part-II: Tele-communication Networks.	VIII	Core	SM (2)	Two Years
6.	KU	1. Introduction to Computers	VI	Core	NSM	Two Years (Pr)
		2. Information and Communication Technology.	V	Core	—	Two Years (Fin)
7.	NU	1. Basics of Information and Communication Technology	VI	Core	NSM	Two Years (Fin)
		2. Computer applications in Libraries.	VII	Core	Two	Years (Fin)
8.	NEHU	1. Introduction to IT.	IX	Core	SM (2)	Two Years
		2. Computer Applications in Library & Information Services	XVI	Core	SM (4)	Two Years
9.	OU	1. Basics of IT in Library	II	Core	NSM	One Year
		2. Computer Applications in	VII	Core	—	—

10. SU	Information Technology	V	Core	NSM	One Year
11. SVU	Introduction to IT	V	Core	NSM	Two Years (Fin)
12. UC	Computer Applications in Libraries & Information Services.	V	Core	NSM	One Year
13. UO	Computer Applications in Library.	V	Elective	NSM	One Year
14. UM	Introduction to IT	III	Core	SM (1)	Two years
15. UU	IT & Computer Applications	IV	Core	NSM	One year

ANNEXURE 2

Table 3. Analysis of Titles of Papers

Sl. No.	Titles of the Paper	Name of the University (S.No.in parentheses refer Table-1)
1.	Application of IT.	AU (1), IGNOU (4).
2.	Introduction to basics of IT.	NEHU (8), OU
3.	IT Part-I. Computer Sciences and Technology	BIT (2), INSDOC (5).
4.	IT Part-II. Applications	BIT (2).
5.	IT Part-II. Telecommunications and Networks.	INSDOC (5)
6.	Introduction to Computers	GU (3), KU (6).
7.	Introduction and communication Technology.	GU (3), KU (6), NU (7).
8.	Computer Applications in Libraries/Information	NU (7), NEHU (8), OU (9) UC (12), UD (13). Centres.
9.	IT and Computer applications	UU (15).

ANNEXURE 3

Table 4. Analysis of Topics

Communication Technology	
Telecommunlcatlon	BIT (12), GU (3), INSDOC (5), KU (6), NU (7), NEHU (8), OU (9), SVU (11), UC (12),
Communication Media	INSDOC (5), OU (9)
Media Technology	BIT (2)
Networks/Working Computer Communications	BIT (2), GU(3), IGNOU (4), INSDOC (5), NU (7), NEHU (8), OU (9), UC (12), UM (14),
Networks, Library Networks Local Area Networks/ Satellite Networks.	UU (15)..
Network Services E-Mail, te l econferencing, Facsimile transmission, Teletext, Video Text, etc.,	BIT (2), GU (3), IGNOU (4), IGNOU (4)
Computer Technology	AU (1), BIT (2), IGNOU (4), INSDOC (5), KU (6), NU(7), NEHU (8), OU (9), UC (12), UM (14), UU (15),
Computer Hardwares	AU (1), INSDOC. (5), KU (6), NU (7), NEHU (8), OU (9), SU (10), SVU (11), U (12), UM (14), UU (15),
Computer Sóftware	AU (1), INSDOC (5), KU (6), NU (7), NEHU (9), OU (9), SU (1O), SVU (11), UC (12), UM (14), UU (15)
Word Processing	OU (9), SVU (1) ..
Programming (Languages)	NEHU (8), SU (10), SVU (11), UC (12), UD (13), UM (14) , UV (15) .,
DBMS	BIT (2), GU (3)., INSDOC (5), KU (6), NEHNU (8), OU (9) .. SVU (11) ,.
Data bases (Bibliographical Factual, and Full Text).	BIT (2), GU (3), IGNOU (4), INSDOC (5), KU (6)
Library Automation (House Keeping Operations, Acquisition Cataloguing and Serial Control)	AU (1) , BIT (2), GU (3), IGNOU (4), INSDOC (5), KU (6), NU (7), OU (9), UU (1.5)
Resource sharing and Networking	INSDOC (5)

Computer based Information	BIT (2), OU (9), UC (12),
Artificial Intelligence Expert Systems, Knowledge Based Systems	AU (1) , GU (3), KU (6) , OU (9), UC (1.2),
Packages	INSDOC (5), NU (7)
Data Processing	AU (1)., NU (7), NEHU (8) , SVU (1 1), UC (12), UM (14), UU (15),
Information Retrievals	OU (9), UU (10),
Audiovisual, Micrographic and Reprographic Technology	GU (3), IGNOUS (4), KU (6), NU (7), NEHU (8), UC (12),
Printing and Publishing Technology.	IGNEOUS (4), UC (12) ... UM (14), UU (1.5).

Facet 4
LIS RESEARCH

10
Importance of Historical Research in Library and Information Science

INTRODUCTION

Research is an honest, intelligent searching for facts and their meaning or implications with reference to a given problem. The product or findings of a given piece of research should be authentic and verifiable contribution to knowledge in the field studied or investigated. The *Webster's Third New International Dictionary* defines research as "studious inquiry or examination, specifically and usually critical and exhaustive investigation or experimentation, having for its aim the discovery of new facts and their i correct interpretation, the revision of accepted conclusions, theories or laws." This definition makes clear the fact that research is not merely 'a search for truth but a prolonged, intensive, purposeful search.

MEANING OF HISTORICAL RESEARCH

Historical method of research is one of the methods employed in all fields of research endeavour especially in social sciences and humanities. Historical research deals with past experience and abstracts whatever generalisation is possible. Its aim is to apply the method of reflective thinking to social problems still unsolved by means of discovery of past trends of event, fact and attitude. It traces lines of development in human thought and action in order to reach some basis for social activity. George. J. Mouly opined that as used by the Greeks, history meant an inquiry designed to construct past events, and in a sense historical research can be defined as a scholarly attempt to discover what has happened. S.P. Sukhia opined that "historical research conducted in the study of any subject denotes an effort to recount some aspects of past life."

TYPES OF HISTORICAL RESEARCH

The historical research can be broadly grouped into the following six types:

1. Biographical research
2. History of institutions and organisations
3. Investigation of sources and influences
4. Editing and translating historical documents
5. Studying the history of ideas, and
6. Compilation of bibliographies

SOURCES OF INFORMATION

To carry out historical research on any aspect, collection of data is very important and essential. The primary sources provide information which lie closest to the historical event. It tends to ensure the integrity of study and strengthen authenticity and reliability. J.L. Bates opined that "primary sources are the raw material of historical interpretation, whereas secondary sources of information provide important information and conceptual development not available elsewhere." Therefore, secondary sources of information are the best tools for filling in the gaps between primary sources of information.

There are several types of documents to be consulted in the

historical method. Archival data is most important of all. Personal documents including life histories of people, public and private documents like diaries, secret files, literature, newspapers, etc. are other important sources of information for those who use historical method. Oral history also forms another important source for writing contemporary history.

PREREQUISITES FOR HISTORICAL RESEARCH

The following prerequisites are very essential for carrying out historical research in any subject or discipline:

1. Knowledge and availability of adequate historical sources of information
2. Selection of relevant and significant historical evidence.
3. Logical sequence of material.
4. Specific plan for acquisition, organisation, storage and retrieval of information.

PROBLEMS IN HISTORICAL RESEARCH

As stated already, research is a studious inquiry or examination in seeking facts and establishment of truth. In the application of any method of research, the researcher encounters certain problems. Historical method is no exception to this fact. The following are some of the important problems in historical research:

1. Deciding how much data is enough. The researcher should be careful to avoid an over-dependence on an insufficient data or evidence.
2. Improper selection of data. The researcher must avoid improper or faulty selection of data.
3. Relying heavily on secondary sources of information.
4. Selection of very broad topic / problem.
5. Failing to evaluate adequately the historical data and their sources, and
6. Failing to interpret data to draw the conclusions.

IMPORTANCE OF HISTORICAL RESEARCH IN LIS

Library and Information Science is one of the disciplines of social sciences. It has a century and half of history. Several stalwarts in the discipline like R.D. Leigh, W.J. Murison, Mumford, W.W. Williamson, G. Spenser, G.S. Bobinstein, J.H. Shera, Shores, McColvin, S.R. Ranganathan and B.S. Kesavan, to mention a few, have greatly contributed to the growth of the subject by applying historical method in their research and publication activity. The importance of historical research is to provide clear perspective of the present and to facilitate planning for the future. C.A. Busha and S.P. Harter were of the opinion that historical research can contribute to the body of knowledge about librarianship and can increase our understanding of how, when and why past events occurred. They further opined that it can expand our appreciation of the significance of these events. Michael Harris stated that "a clear understanding of historical definition of the functions of the libraries may well contribute to increased communication between libraries." Emphasising the need for and importance of historical research, J.H. Shera stated: "Library history allows librarians to better understanding the present and to more effectively fulfil their social responsibility." Commenting on the state of library history in India, Donald G. Davis advocated the promotion of historical writing in the field of Library and Information Science. He further stated that "Indian library history is a subject that excites the imagination because of its long duration, rich primary resources and vast potential for significant study. Yet one can be frustrated not only by the problems of library development in India, but by the status of describing and evaluating that development with historical perspective."

In short, historical research can help the researchers, teachers of LIS, practicing librarians and information specialists to carry out research by applying historical method and present past events in an efficient and effective manner and also not to repeat past mistakes in the contemporary developments in Library and Information Science.

HISTORICAL RESEARCH IN LIBRARY AND INFORMATION STUDIES IN USA AND GREAT BRITAIN

United States of America has shown the way for others in the application of historical method in Library and Information Science research. Some of the important historical research works in LIS are quoted for information. In 1943, G. Spenser in his work entitled *Chicago Public Library: Origin and Backgrounds* traced the development of Chicago Public Library. J.H. Shera in 1949 studied the origins of the public library movement in New England from 1629-1885. F.G. Collier in his doctoral dissertation submitted to Harvard University in 1952 studied the history of American Public Library Movement through 1880. In 1956, Walter M. Whitchell traced hundred years history of Boston Public Library. George S. Bobinski in 1959 studied the history and impact of American Public library development. W.W. Williamson in 1963 studied the contributions of William Frederick Poole for the development of modern library movement. These are some of the best examples of application of historical research.

Likewise the contributions of British researchers and authors in the application of historical method in library research is significant and far-reaching, Some of the important historical research works in Library and Information Science are quoted for information D.M. Norris traced the history of cataloguing. J. Thomson in his classic works dealt on the history of principles of librarianship. J.L. Thornton edited and presented selected readings in history of librarianship. W.J. Murison traced the origin, purpose and significance of public library in Great Britain.

HISTORICAL RESEARCH IN LIBRARY AND INFORMATION SCIENCE STUDIES IN INDIA

During the past six decades, several research scholars for obtaining formal M.Phil. and Ph.D. degrees from the universities and authors applied historical method in their research pursuits or in their writings to trace the growth and development of various types of libraries, library movement and library services. Several studies have been undertaken on different facets of history of libraries in India covering pre- and post-Independent India. One of the earliest efforts in this direction is N.M. Dutta's work entitled "History of Indian Libraries From Earlier Times to the Present Day", an article published in *Modern Librarian* in 1932. Mr Dutta in his article lamented the lack of interest or writing on the subject. O.P. Sharma in his article based on his dissertation "Literature on the History of Library Movement in India", pointed out continuing lack of interest in Indian library historical writings. K. Ramakrishna Rao in his article "Library Development in India" attempted to place the topic in the context of historical and social factors. Anis Khursid in his article "Growth of Libraries in India" concentrated on the history of libraries during the past two centuries. A.K. Mukherji's work *Librarianship, Its History and Philosophy*, S.K. Mukherji's *Development of Libraries and Library Science in India* and D.N. Marshall's work *History of Libraries: Ancient and Medieval* dealt with critical evaluation of the position of libraries and their functions in ancient, medieval and modern India. S.N. Sadhu and B.N. Saraf in their work *Library Legislation in India: A Historical and Comparative Study* have dealt the genesis and development of library legislation in India. P.N. Kaula's work *Library Movement In India*, G.L. Trehan's work *Modern Public Library Movement in India* and M.L. Nagar's work *Foundations of Library Movement in India* have critically evaluated the genesis, growth and spread of library movement in India. Jogesh Mishra's work *History of Libraries and Librarianship in Modern India Since 1850* attempts to present historical development of libraries in India. Likewise, R.K. Bhatt's work *A Historical Study of the Growth and Development of Libraries in Modern India (1901-1985), With Special Reference to Delhi, Agra*, critically examines development of libraries in Delhi and Agra regions of Northern India.

Donald G. Davis commenting on the status of library historiography in India writes: "Although a core of literature on Indian library historiography exists, it has many imbalances and gaps. The scholars are very dispersed in their interests and their geographical location with one person rarely contributing more than one work. There is little pattern to existing research efforts. The one obsession appears to be pre-occupation with legislation and implementation of authorisation for public libraries to the exclusion of other libraries in their role in national culture."

Of late, the situation has been changing. Many historical studies have been carried out on growth and development of college and university libraries in post-Independent India.

Andhra Pradesh carved out a special place in the history of library movement and development of public libraries for the entire country. Many studies applying historical method have been carried out by the scholars and researchers. Mention may be made of K. Sarada's work *Andhra Pradesh Library Association* which traces the genesis, development and activities of the Association. V. Venkatappaiah applied historical method profusely to trace the library movement in Andhra and Telangana regions. A.A.N. Raju's work on *History of Library Movement in Andhra Pradesh (1900-1956)* is another best example of application of historical method. In this work an attempt has been made for an indepth study of history of library movement in Coastal Andhra and Telangana regions of Andhra Pradesh on the basis of select case studies.

VALUE OF LIBRARY HISTORY

By applying historical method, the researcher traces genesis and development and activities of institutions, societies and individuals. In other words, it is the history of institutions, societies and individuals. This method enables us to trace and present history of various types of libraries which can be called library history or history of libraries.

Library history has one main function to perform. It is to offer broad principles and generate gateways of historical truth. Library history is essential if we are to understand current library situations and how all has come to be what is now. Library history also offers us a contrast which enables us to appreciate the present system by a study of the past. Existing library systems like our present social, political and economic conditions are the result of the factors that precede them. So a knowledge of what has happened in the past is very essential for us to progress into the future, avoiding mistakes of our predecessors, adopting methods that have proved successful and pursuing paths that have been blazed for our guidance with the object of extending them further towards our goal.

CONCLUSION

In the light of preceding presentation, it may be concluded that there is a vital scope for the application of historical method in Library and Information Science research. The examples cited amply demonstrate the importance of historical method. There is a continuing need for historical method of research in LIS. Historical research interprets past trends of attitude, event and fact and helps to find trends and developments of various aspects of libraries and information centres. It is incumbent on the part of researchers and authors to apply this method in their research pursuits and enrich historical studies in Library and Information Science.

11
Research and Publication Activity in the Departments of Library and Information Science

INTRODUCTION

Libraries and Information Centres play a very important role in expansion and development of education, research and socio-economic development of a nation. The phenomenal growth in the universe of knowledge resulting in 'Information explosion' and 'Inter-disciplinary approach' to research during the past two decades generated new demands on the services provided by the libraries and information centers. The rapid strides the country has made in different spheres of national endeavour during the past three decades and the efforts being made to sustain this progress added new dimension for the information services rendered by the Library and Information Centres.

To fulfill the information needs of various categories of

clientele viz Scientists, Researchers, Scholars, Educationists, Engineers, Technologists, and even common man, pinpointedly, exhaustively and expeditiously, Libraries and Information Centres must be properly equipped and managed by well trained library personnel. To train the personnel for efficient management of libraries and information centres, the departments which train the personnel had to play a pivotal role in providing right type of education and training to the entrants of the profession. It is the duty of the Departments to be abreast with new developments. It also enables them to specialize in different areas of Library and Information Science. As a result, teachers will be in a better position to impart current thought to the students and thereby achieve higher professional standards.

NEED FOR RESEARCH

Research is a "Studious inquiry or examination especially critical and exhaustive investigation or experimentation having for its aim the discovery of new facts and their correct interpretation, the revision of accepted conclusions, theories or laws in the light of newly discovered facts, theories or laws.[1] Research is not merely search for truth, but prolonged intensive and purposeful search. Research in any discipline helps in its growth and ensures new developments. It extends the frontiers of knowledge and makes it possible for new interpretation and application of existing knowledge. It also develops individual personality and scholarship and brings recognition in the world of learning and achievement.

Library and Information Science education is no exception to this. The Library Science Departments in the Universities must promote research and developmental activities so as to contribute to the sumtotal of knowledge. The rapid scientific, industrial and technological advancements the country has made resulted in the growth of number of special libraries and advanced information centres attached to Research and Development (R&D) wings of the Industrial and Technological centres. Research has to be under taken for indepth study of these special libraries and information centres for studying their organisational setup, services and the type of trained personnel they need for managing their libraries and information centres. On the basis of results of research, special courses can be introduced in our M Lib I Sc and other higher programmes. Neelameghan[2] has highlighted the need for the promotion of research by the Information Science School so as to make "Useful contribution to the advancement of the subject and thereby to the advancement of society, play a leadership role in directing developments in the field, and present to society a proper image of the capabilities and potentialities of information science and service".

Teaching and research must be regarded as the two inseparable components of university education. The slogan 'Publish or Perish' rightly applies to teachers in Library Science for their career development. It also helps indirectly for the growth of knowledge and thereby to project the image of the Department brightly to the out-side world.

PRESENT POSITION OF RESEARCH

Library Science Education has developed significantly after independence. At present there are 44 University Departments and other institutions conducting Bachelor and Master's Degree courses in the subject. Krishna Kumar and Sardhana[3] while surveying the status of research in Library and Information Science in Indian Library Schools, listed research barriers, objectives, duration and contents of M Phil and Ph D programmes and suggested areas of research with special reference to India.

As regards research courses leading to M Phil/Ph D programmes, nine departments viz Andhra, Banaras, Bombay, Delhi, Karnataka, Mysore, Punjab, Rajasthan and Vikram have facilities for doing research leading to the award of Ph. D degree. All these Universities including Osmania conduct Masters Degree Programme. None of the Departments, excepting Delhi, offer courses leading to the award of M Phil degree. As per the survey[4] referred to earlier 23 candidates had registered for doctoral programmes in six library schools. When compared with other disciplines, even in the field of Social Sciences, the research activity in the departments of Library & Information Science is not encouraging. There are various reasons for this slow progress.

REASONS FOR SLOW PROGRESS IN RESEARCH

Following reasons may be attributed for the slow progress of research in the Departments :

1. The courses in Library Science viz Dip Lib Sc/B Lib Sc were initially started as part-time courses depending mostly on part-time teachers. In certain cases even the full time courses were run by part-time teachers. This has effected the growth of the full fledged faculty in the Departments. This situation is still continuing in certain cases for various reasons.
2. The teacher-student ratio is not satisfactory. Due to lack of sufficient teaching staff, a staff member is obliged to teach 3 or 4 courses which is rather a difficult task for oneself to keep abreast with latest trends in these subject fields and finds no time for pusuit of research.
3. Teaching of several subjects and taking more classes than the normal workload also effects one's abilities for concentration and specialization in the subject areas.
4. Many a time faculty members are charged with administrative routine, conducting of examinations, invigilation work which come in the way for fruitful use of their leisure time for research pursuits.
5. Lack of proper financial support for undertaking research projects and in certain cases lack of support from the higher echelons in the university administration has been hindering the genesis and growth of research.
6. The 'big brother' attitude of the developed departments in the university setup and allocation of larger amounts for

research in sciences is also one of the reasons for this slow progress.

7 Absence of 'research tradition', with few exceptions, and lack of recognised supervisors is coming in the way of young and energetic faculty members to undertake research.

AREAS OF RESEARCH

Ranganathan[5] has listed the problems for persuit of research in the idea plane, verbal plane and notional plane in classification and problems in retrieval with computer. The UGC Review Committee on Library Science[6] has also identified sectors for research. These sectors include : 1 Classification, 2 Cataloguing, 3 Documentation, 4 Reprography, 5 Translation of research papers, 6 Book Science, 7 Standards for Library process, 8 Library Organisation, 9 Public Library Finance, 10 Academic Library System and Special Library System. Krishna Kumar and Sardhana[7], on the basis of information they collected from the library schools, listed the areas in which the research is being under taken. These include — 1 Classification and Cataloguing, 2 Biblio graphic Control, 3 Administration and Management, 4 Library Legislation, 5 Indexing, 6 National Information System, 7 Man power requirements, 8 University Libraries, 9 Users studies and 10 Growth of Knowledge.

These topics covet the 'traditional' areas of Library Science. It would be better if the research is directed towards inter-disciplinary studies like library movement and their impact on social and cultural development of society, library and information science education, users education, role of libraries in the spread of education, and computer applications in library operation. John Dean[8] identified : 1 Library standards (Buildings, staff, stocks), 2 Automation, 3 Bibliographical research and 4 Cataloguing and classification as the areas for profitable exploration. He has also suggested two streams of research activity.

PUBLICATION ACTIVITY OF THE DEPARTMENTS

The results of a particular piece of research must be published for wider circulation so that the fellow research workers can know what is going on in a particular field. Retrospective research is being reported in the bibliography of dissertations/ theses accepted by the Indian Universities published by the Association of Indian Universities. This tool is confined to the research degrees awarded by Indian Universities. Current research which is being done by the Departments on project undertaken by them individually must also needs publication. Documentation Research and Training Centre (DRTC), Bangalore, one of the foremost institutions in the country has been continuously engaged in research in the field of Library and Information Science. The result of research is being reported through its organ *Library Science with slant to Documentation*. Few library science departments have their departmental journals through which the contributions of their staff members are published. Mention may be made of *Libra* (Rajasthan), *Timeless Fellowship* (Karnataka), *Journal of Library & Information Science* (Delhi) and the latest to join this group is *"Progress of Library & Information Science"* Banaras). Some of these journals also publish research articles contributed by the faculty members of other Library Science Departments in country. The Department of Library and Information Science. University of Madras through its 'DELSIUM' reports (mimeographed) is able to inform the research activity of its faculty members. Information is not available about the publication activity of other departments.

FINANCIAL ASPECTS

Providing necessary financial support is one of the pre-requisites for embarking upon research work. Enthusiasm, zeal and ability for doing research has no meaning unless the research is made free from financial problems during the period of research. Agencies like UGC, ICHR, ICSSR, ICAR, ICMR, Planning Commission, Department of Science and Technology Government of India and individual Universities are funding the research projects carried out in the country. But their support for research activity in Library & Information Science is not very encouraging. UGC under its 'Assistance to Special Programmes and Research' has been assisting financially to : 1 College Science Improvement Programme (COSIP), 2 College Humanities and Social Science Improvement Programme (COHSIP), 3 University Leadership Projects, 4 Faculty Improvement Programme (FIP), 5 Support to individual, Group and Departmental Research Programmes, 6 Adult and continuing education Programmes, 7 Special assistance programmes to select Departments and 8 Centres of Advanced study.

Most of these programmes are directed towards sciences and also to certain extent to 'major' disciplines in social sciences. The support to Library Sciences Departments either for faculty improvent or for the development of research activity is not satisfactory. Even for the award of Junior/Senior Research Fellowship, Library Science Departments get least priority. These fellowship programmes are meant for M Phil/Ph D programmes and since majority of the Departments of Library Science have not yet introduced these courses. They are at a disadvantageous position to claim for these fellowships.

FUTURE COURSE OF ACTION

The progress of research and publication activity in the Departments need encouragement and financial support from UGC and other funding agencies referred to in para 6. For proper growth and development of research and publication activity in the Departments, the following measures are suggested for accelerated growth and development of research and publication activity in Library and Information Science.

1. UGC through its several developmental programmes specially through FIP and Special Assistance Programmes must support the 'developing' departments of Library and Information Science to initiate research programmes.

2. The Departments, with the financial support from the UGC take initiative for the creation of 'Research cells' for undertaking research projects.
3. The post of 'Research Assistants' must be created in the Departments, so as to assist the faculty members in their research pursuits.
4. There is a dearth for recognised supervisors in the Depart ments, to guide the young faculty members for undertaking research work, and therefore interdisciplinary subjects may be chosen for research to utilize the services of recognised supervisors from the other disciplines.
5. The Seminar on Library & Information Science Education in Indian held in 1977 recommended that the funding agencies (referred to in para 6) may be requested to include Library and Information Science as a subject of their purview for award of scholarships, fellow ships, Associateships etc and grants for projects for individual or team research. Vigorous efforts should be made to realize this objective.
6. The Departments of Library & Information Science in the country must take necessary steps to start an annual publication (at least mimeographed) to communicate research activity of the faculty members. Kaula[10] has emphasised the need for bringing to the notice of the professionals the work of 'Research Cells' through Departmental publications.
7. Appointment of 'Professor Emeritus' in the 'developing' Departments for inculcating 'research temper' in the minds of young faculty members and guiding them in their research pursuits will go a long way in the developments of research activity.

CONCLUSION

The research and publication activity of the Library Science Departments in the county deserve encouragement and support.

Cooperation among the Departments is very essential for promoting research and publication activities. There are certain Departments which need strengthening of the faculty. The Library Science Education Advisory Committee of the UGC must lend a helping hand in this respect for assisting the developing' Departments. Once the faculty is strengthened it may slowly lead to the promotion of research and publication activity. It is hoped that during the VI Plan period, research programmes of the Departments will receive necessary financial support. UGC and other funding agencies must come forward for the promotion of research and publication activity of the Library & Information Science Departments in the country.

REFERENCES

1. WEBSTERS THIRD New International Dictionary. 1961. London. G Bell. P 1930.
2. NEELAMEGHAN (A) : Guide lines for formulation of a policy on education, training and development of Library and Information Science personnel. (Paper presented to the seminar on Library and Information Science Education, Delhi, October 3-8,1977. P 41).
3. KRISHNA KUMAR and SARDHANA (JL) : Research in Library and Information Science in Indian Library Schools. (Paper presented 1o the Seminar on Library and Information Science Education in India. Delhi, October 3-8, 1977. P 6).
4. Ibid. P6.
5. RANGANATHAN(SR): Prolegomena to Library Classification. Ed3. 1967. Bombay, Asia Publishing House. P 591-594.
6. UNIVERSITY GRANTS (Commission) (India), LIBRARY SCIENCE IN INDIAN UNIVERSITIES (Review Committee on—) (1965) : Report. New Delhi, UGC. P 29-33.
7. KRISHNA KUMAR and SARDHANA (JL) : Op cit. P 8.
8. DEAN (John) : Planning Library Education Programmes. 1972. London. Andre Deutsch. P 91-93.
9. LIBRARY AND INFORMATION SCIENCE EDUCATION IN INDIA (Seminar on—) (Delhi) (1977) : Recommendations. P 4-5.
10. KAULA (PN) : Editorial (In *Progress of Library and Information Science.* 1. 1980. P 2).

12
LIS Research in India: Trends and Development

INTRODUCTION

Libraries and information centres play a vital role in the socio-economic development of a nation. The accelerated growth in R&D activities in science and technology and other fields of human endeavour contributed to a phenomenal growth in the universe of subjects, resulting in information explosion and inter-disciplinary approach to research during the past seven decades. These developments generated new demands on the services offered by libraries and information centres.

The rapid strides our country made in the different spheres of national endeavour since Independence, and the efforts being made to sustain this progress and attain new heights added new dimensions to the services rendered by libraries and information centres. In order to meet the new challenges, to find proper and suitable solutions and to investigate new areas, research has become one of the most important and essential aspects of Library and Information Science (LIS). *The Webster's Third New International Dictionary* defines research as "studious inquiry or examination; specifically and usually critical and exhaustive investigation or experimentation, having for its aim the discovery of new facts and their correct interpretation, the revision of accepted conclusions, theories or laws." Research is essential to examine the existing situations and problems and find out new solutions. It is a means to the advancement of any subject/ discipline, LIS being no exception.

NEED FOR LIS RESEARCH

The following factors have prompted the need for research in LIS :

1. Changes in the information environment in the country due to socio-economic developments naturally necessitate a fresh outlook on the discipline.
2. Research at advanced level is very essential for the progress/ advancement of LIS as a discipline. This is because research programmes can sharpen the existing tools and techniques and design new ones. These research activities/programmes help train the required manpower who can, in turn, take up research work for further advancement.
3. In order to find solutions to the problems faced in the management of library and information centres, the librarians/information officers should qualify themselves by obtaining research degrees that enable them to undertake critical and exhaustive inquiries pertaining to library and information centres.
4. The UGC is insisting on research qualifications for teachers of LIS and librarians working in senior positions in academic libraries.
5. For recruitment to senior positions in special and technical libraries, the employers insist on research degrees for the candidates.
6. Research degrees have become essential to acquire status, recognition and prestige.
7. Research qualifications provide strong initiative for the satisfaction of personal vanity and intellectual need.

8. In order to get the same status and pay scales as those of teachers of LIS, library professionals working in college and university libraries must acquire similar qualifications.

GENESIS OF LIS RESEARCH IN INDIA

The genesis and development of LIS research in India may be traced back to 1924 when Dr. S.R.Ranganathan appeared on the scene. His seminal contributions to various facets of librarianship enriched the discipline and elevated it from an art into a science. He was primarily responsible for introducing university level courses in our country. He started under-graduate level courses in LIS for the first time at the University of Madras in 1931. Later, in 1937, this course was upgraded to P.G. Diploma in LIS. After India attained Independence, many universities in the country slowly started introducing LIS courses.

At present, there are nearly 80 to 100 universities in the country having LIS departments offering BLISc/MLISc courses, and about forty universities offering MPhil/PhD programmes. The credit of introducing a doctoral programme in LIS for the first time in the country goes to Dr. S.R.Ranganathan. He introduced the programme in 1950 at the University of Delhi. Dr. D.B. Krishna Rao was the first scholar to obtain the PhD degree in LIS from the University of Delhi in 1957, under the guidance of Dr. S.R.Ranganathan. The topic for his research was *"Facet Analysis and Depth Classification of Agriculture "*.

For nearly two decades, no other university in the country seems to have either introduced a PhD programme or conferred a Ph.D. degree. It was Punjab University, Chandigarh, which turned out the second Ph.D. scholar in India. Dr. Pandey S.K. Sharma obtained Ph.D. in LIS in 1977 from this university. His topic was *"Expansion and Modification of DDC (18th Edn.)* for *Classifying Indological Books"*. At present, between 30 and 40 university LIS departments in the country are offering MPhil/PhD programmes. The exact number of scholars registered for these programmes in the various LIS departments is not available.

Unfortunately, this is also the case with regard to the number of candidates who actually obtained MPhil/PhD degrees from the different universities in India since 1950.

LIS RESEARCH OUTPUT

It has been estimated that until 1985, about 1000 trend reports/project reports/literature surveys for obtaining MLISc degrees and 18 dissertations for MPhil degrees and 58 doctoral theses for PhD degrees have been produced. A break up of doctoral dissertations on various facets of LIS from January 1980 to June 1991 is given in Table 1 on the following page.

Table 1

S.No.	Name of the Broad Topic	No of Ph.Ds
1.	Library Co-operation	2
2.	Management	7
3.	Information Storage and Retrieval	2
4.	Organisation	3
5.	Reference & Information Sources & Services	6
6.	Classification	5
7.	Marathi	5
8.	Hindi	1
9.	Development of Periodical Literature	1
10.	LIS Education	2
11.	Special Libraries	3
12.	Public Libraries	6
13.	University Libraries	12
14.	History of Conditions	2
15.	Library Movement & Library Legislation	1
16	Library Buildings	1
17.	Citation Analysis and Bibliometrics	3
18.	Information Systems & Networks	7
19.	User Studies	4
20.	Library Collection Management	1
21.	Thesaurus	1
22.	Content Analysis	1

As regards doctoral dissertations (PhDs) it has been estimated that between the years 1950 and 1997, 293 research scholars have been awarded doctorates out of which 264 awards were in US and the rest of 29 were in disciplines other than LIS The maximum number of doctorates 48 were awarded in 1992 (the centenary years of Dr S.R. Ranganathan). In 1991 and 1994, 29 candidates received doctoral degrees each year. In 1989, 24 candidates were awarded doctorate degrees.

BIBLIOGRAPHICAL CONTROL OF LIS RESEARCH IN INDIA

There is a need to have effective bibliographic control of LIS research m India so as to provide its true picture to the LIS profession. The following published tools and professional journals provide us information about output of LIS research in India.

Completed Doctoral Research

A Bibliography of Doctoral Dissertations Accepted by Indian Universities 1857-1970-Social Sciences (Inter-University Board of India [now named as Association of Indian Universities], New Delhi, 1974) is the only source for complete doctoral dissertations in LIS. In addition, the *University News*, under its heading 'Theses of the Month' announces the doctoral degrees awarded by Indian universities. Besides the newsletters/communications issued by ILA, IASLIC and 1ATLIS also report award of PhD degrees in LIS.

Research in Progress

Information about 'Research in Progress' is also reported in some professional journals like *Herald of Library Science, Indian Journal of Library and Information Science, Indian Journal of Information, Library and Society* and also newsletters issued by ILA, IASLIC and IATLIS. Bibliographic control and dissemination of research work in progress and published helps the prospective LIS researchers in many ways. It enables to know the trends and developments, and the emerging thrust areas.

REASONS FOR SLOW PROGRESS IN LIS RESEARCH

Even though nearly hundred LIS schools offer courses in LIS of which about fifty offer Master's, M.Phil. and Ph.D programmes, the progress in this respect is not encouraging. The important reasons for this slow progress may be as follows:

1. Lack of research experience in the faculty. The situation is fast changing for the better.
2. Absence of knowledge about research methodology among the prospective researchers and in some cases supervisors.
3. Faculty burdened with teaching and in many of the LIS schools poor faculty strength.
4. Non-availability of required, qualified and recognised research guides/supervisors.
5. Inadequate and in some cases lack of financial support.
6. Lack of good library/computer laboratory facilities and services.
7. Inadequate or lack of incentives to doctoral degree holders.
8. Problems in identification of research topics/areas.

The above mentioned constraints can be overcome by encouraging research among the faculty members by way of undertaking major and minor research projects for which financial support is offered by UGC, CSIR, ICSSR and other funding agencies Incentives and facilities should be provided to the faculty for undertaking research themselves and also by encouraging youngsters who have aptitude for research.

AGENCIES WHICH SUPPORT LIS RESEARCH

Most of the LIS research carried out in Indian LIS schools is personal in nature; the primary objective of research scholars is to get research degrees for their personal promotion and satisfaction. Institutional research in LIS has not received the attention it deserves. We do not have a separate national agency or apex body which is exclusively devoted to support of LIS research. But, there are a few national agencies, institutions and government departments which support LIS research. Mention may be made of bodies like UGC, ICSSR and RRRLF which support LIS research. In addition to these bodies, other agencies like CSIR, ICAR, ICMR, NCERT and Planning Commission, Government of India should also come forward to support LIS research.

RESEARCH IN LIS DURING THE PAST 5 YEARS

An attempt has been made to look into the state of LIS research carried out in the Indian universities for obtaining PhD degrees during the past five years, i.e. from 1993 to October 1997. The primary source for this exercise is *University News*, brought out by the Association of Indian Universities (AIU). All the universities, including deemed universities and institutions of higher learning, send their communications of award of research degrees of the qualified candidates for publication in the *University News*. To analyse and assess the topics registered for doctoral degrees, and also the doctoral theses actually accepted by the Indian universities, *University News* has been scanned from Vol.31 (1993) to Vol.35 (Oct. 1997). The following sections briefly deal with the results of the analysis and assessment on the basis of facts and figures gathered from this primary source.

NUMBER OF CANDIDATES OBTAINING DOCTORAL DEGREES

On the basis of the data gathered from *University News*, we find that 87 candidates have obtained Ph.D. degrees during the past five years, i.e. between 1993 and October 1997. The year-wise break-up is 17 (1993), 19 (1994), 23 (1995), 13 (1996) and 15 (1997). Among the several areas of research, "User Studies" occupies the prime position as a favourite. Seventeen scholars have obtained their doctoral degrees selecting the different aspects of "User Studies". This is followed by University Libraries (11), Bibliometrics (9), Information Storage and Retrieval (8), Management (7), Public Libraries (7), and Information Centres/ Services/Systems and Networks (6).

ANALYSIS OF DOCTORAL THESES

The focus of research under "User Studies" includes: attitudes, information-seeking behaviour of university teachers, botanists, social scientists, economists, fisheries scientists, women teachers and medical and para-medical professionals. The narrower topics under "University Libraries" include: planning, development, evaluation of services, finance, New Educational Policy, personnel, organisational structure, collection development, development of university libraries in Andhra Pradesh, Madhya Pradesh and Punjab. The specific areas under "Bibliometrics" include: assessment of agriculture literature output, use pattern of literature in economics and bio-sciences, analysis of literature in social sciences, horticulture, literature, analysis of science journals, nuclear science productivity, and analysis of doctoral dissertations. The focus of research under "Information Storage and Retrieval Systems" includes: rural information systems, nutrition, health sciences and laser technology. The sub-areas under "Management" include: development, services, impact on the community and public library system in Orissa. The other broad areas under which research work has been carried out include: cataloguing, computerisation, community information, indexing, information management, library legislation, library history, library profession, library associations, marketing of information, national libraries, reference tools and sources, school libraries, and special libraries.

CONCLUSION

In the preceding paras, an attempt has been made to present the state of LIS research in the country during the past five years based on the data gathered from *University News*. Research in LIS is slowly but steadily progressing right from 1970s to reach new heights. Thanks to LIS departments in the universities, many young and enthusiastic research scholars and practising young librarians are coming forward to utilise the research fellowship offered by UGC and pursue research for obtaining doctoral degrees. In addition to UGC, national agencies like ICSSR, ICMR, ICAR, DST, CSIR, ICHR, ICCR and other funding agencies should come forward in a big way to offer scholarships/fellowships/travel grants to accelerate LIS research in the country. The LIS departments in the country should be strengthened with required and qualified faculty and infrastructure facilities like computer laboratories, on-line search, E-Mail facilities to guide the research scholars by the faculty members. It is hoped that in the 21st century and in the context of emerging Information Society, LIS research in the country will attain new heights.

REFERENCES

1. Raju, A.A.N. A Look Into LIS Research in India During the Past Five Years, IN *Fifty Years of LIS Education in India*. Ed. By A.A.N. Raju, et al. Hyderabad, Suchithritha Graphics, 1997, pp. 186-198.
2. *DESIDOC Bulletin of Information Technology*. V 18, N 1, Jan 1998 (Special issue on Research in LIS.)

13

Prerequisites for LIS Teaching and Research in Telugu at the University Level

INTRODUCTION

Library and Information Science (LIS) is an emerging and expanding professional discipline. During the course of its 120 years of chequered history, the discipline absorbed into its fold both traditional as well as the newly emerging Information and Communication technologies. This is but natural for any discipline to meet the changing needs of the society. The emergence of "Information Society"cast a new role and responsibility for those who are actively involved in teaching, research and publication activity in LIS.

LANGUAGE POLICY

Courses at different levels in LIS are being offered by the LIS Schools and/or Departments in the Universities, Institutions and Library Associations, all over the world. In our country most of the LIS Schools in the Universities have been offering UG/PG/

Research Courses mostly in English. The Education Commissions appointed by Government of India in the past viz., Radhakrishnan Commission and Kothari Commission have emphasised the need for teaching and research in regional languages at the University level.

The Government of Andhra Pradesh long back has enunciated its policy to use Telugu not only in its administration but also as a medium of instruction at the UG and PG levels. As a consequence to this policy the State Government established/ supported Telugu medium colleges or sections in the existing colleges to offer courses in Arts, Social Sciences and Sciences at the undergraduate level throughout the State. But not much progress has been achieved to use Telugu as medium of instruction at the PG level.

PREREQUISITES

LIS courses at UG/PG level is being offered by the Universities in the State during the past three decades. But efforts have not been made to teach LIS in Telugu even at the UG level. LIS being a professional course, its teaching in Telugu at the University level and carrying out research and publication is very much dependent on the following prerequisites.

LIS Glossaries

It is well known fact the most of us depend on the literature available on LIS in English for teaching, publication and Research. To bring out the required reading materials such as text-books, reference books, monographs and for writing articles in Telugu and for translating books from say English to Telugu we require glossaries of LIS terms from English to Telugu. It is true that the need for standard and authoritative glossary of LIS terms in Telugu is being acutely felt by the professionals and authors who are engaged in enriching LIS literature in Telugu.

Bringing out standard and authoritative glossaries covering the traditional as well as emerging areas in LIS is sine quo non for bringing out the required reading materials in Telugu. It is not out of place to mention here the efforts that have been made in the past by the institutions and individuals. The first and foremost Institution in this respect is the Telugu Academy, which has brought out a number of glossaries covering important subject fields which may be of use to LIS professionals. These include: Glossary of Administrative Terms (1980), and Provisional List of Technical Terms from English to Telugu covering Arts and Social Sciences: Logic, Philosophy, Psychology, Linguistics, History, Political Science, Public Administration, Sociology, Anthropology, Economics, Commerce and Geography and Sciences: Geology, Mathematics, Physics, Chemistry, Botany, Zoology and Home Science. These glossaries will help us to bring out LIS glossaries from English to Telugu and for translation of schedules of classification schemes into Telugu and also books from English to Telugu. Telugu Akademi has also taken a project to bring out glossary of LIS terms from English-Telugu. The project has long back completed and awaits publication. Another Project in the pipeline is to bring out definitions and explanations with examples for each word already approved by the Akademi. The author of this paper has closely associated with this project.

The Telugu University, Hyderabad had in the past approved a proposal to bring out glossary of LIS terms from English to Telugu. A provisional list of terms prepared by the experts including the author of this Paper on important areas of LIS was submitted for consideration. But the said proposal has not come through so far for known or unknown reasons.

In addition to Institutions, individuals have also played a prominent role in bringing out LIS glossaries. Mention may be made of the contributions of Dr. Velaga Venkatappayya, Paturi Vijaya Kumar and Prof. P. Soma Raju, who have brought out glossaries of LIS from English to Telugu.

Text-books and Other Reading Materials

The required reading materials such as text books,

monographs and reference books is another important prerequisite for teaching LIS at the Universities. In order to supplement and compliment class-room teaching, the students require the reading materials both at UG/PG levels.

In the past, efforts have been made by the institutions and individuals to bring out text books and monographs to meet the requirements of UG level students (i.e. CLISc/BLISc). To state again, the Telugu Akademi has taken initiative in bringing out UG level text books. It has published text books covering the papers taught in BLISc Courses of the universities in the State. These text-books cover Library and Society, Library Administration/ Management,Classification (Theory & Practice), Cataloguing (Theory & Practice), Bibliography and Documentation. The textbook on Reference Sources and Services is yet to be published. The Staff members from the Universities in the State have closely associated in editing/writing these text books.

Mention may be made of the individuals like Dr. V. Venkatappayya, Paturi Vijaya Kumar, K.Ramachander Rao, and Prof.P.Kamaiah, who brought out a number of text books, monographs and lecture notes on their own to meet the requirements of CLISc/BLISc Students.

The A.P.Library Association under the authorship of Sri Paturi Nagabhusanam, brought a number of publications in Telugu which are of use to students of LIS.

Periodical Literature

Periodical literature in Telugu is equally important to supplement the macro literature and also to encourage research and publication activity in Telugu. Till now there is no exclusive Research journal in LIS in Telugu to act as a forum/medium for publication of articles and research reports, etc. The existing Telugu periodical *Grandhalaya Sarvaswamu* has been doing yeomen service for those interested to write on LISc in Telugu. But its level and coverage needs to be improved. Mention also be made of the journal being brought out by Telugu Akademi entitled

Telugu monthly which acted as forum for those authors who write in Telugu on LISc. But of late the format, coverage and frequency of this journal has been changed leaving less scope for writing articles in Social Sciences including LIS.

Therefore, there is a need for a research journal which can exclusively deal with LIS and encourage publication of research articles in Telugu. The Telugu University may consider this suggestion to bring out a half yearly journal or an annual volume to start with in LIS.

Qualified Teachers

Besides the requisite reading materials, qualified teachers in LIS is another prerequisite for teaching LIS in the Universities. In addition to Academic/Professional qualifications, as prescribed by the UGC, proficiency in Telugu language and contributors in Telugu on LIS may be prescribed as additional and desirable qualifications. Efforts have to be made to teach LIS in Telugu to start with at the BLISc level in the Universities in the State. This will give an opportunity and needed experience to those who presently teach LIS in English at the University Library Schools.

Commissioning Translations

In addition to bringing out text-books and monographs in Telugu on LISc at U.G. level to start with, there is a need for translation of standard works in English into Telugu. The translation may include cover to cover/theme/free translations. The institution/university intends to start LIS courses in Telugu may commission those teachers/authors who have the requisite experience in translation and subject knowledge/expertise for translating authoritative and standard works into Telugu.

Compilation of Retrospective Bibliography of LIS Literature in Telugu

The literature on LIS in Telugu is not that impressive to be compared with Hindi, Malayalam, and Bengali. Nevertheless few enthusiastic authors have been publishing books and articles in

Telugu News Papers and Journals. An attempt has to be made to compile a retrospective bibliography of books, articles, conference reports, translations, directories, and reference material if any, from 1914 i.e. the year of establishment of A.P. Library Association, till to date. This bibliography if compiled and published, will give us an idea of the literature so far published in Telugu on various aspects of LIS and also useful to the students, teachers and practicing librarians. The Telugu Univer-sity/Telugu Akademi/ ICSSR Southern Regional Centre at Hyderabad may be approached to undertake this project or assist financially to those who may take up this as a project for compilation.

DISTANCE EDUCATION (DE) - COURSE MATERIAL:

The Distance Education Institutions/Universities in the country have been offering courses on LIS. The course material brought out by IGNOU for BLISc/MLISc courses and Dr.B.R.Ambedkar Open University course material for BLISc Courses is worth consideration for translating in to Telugu. This requires institutional agreements. The School of Distance Learning and Continuing Education (SDLCE) Kakatiya University, Warangal has brought out course material in Telugu at CLISc level.

CONCLUSION

The important prerequisites viz. Glossaries, text books and other reading materials, periodical literature, qualified teachers, commissioning translations, translation of DE Course material and compilation of retrospective Bibliography of LIS literature in Telugu discussed in the preceding sections will greatly contribute to embark upon LIS teaching and research at the University level. The materials so far produced by the Institutions and individuals have been to certain extent meeting the requirements of those BLISc students who are studying the course in English either in the traditional or distance mode and writing the examinations in Telugu. Some more literature on LIS in Telugu has to be brought out if any Institution is thinking of starting a course at UG level. Introduction of Telugu as medium of instruction and research in

LIS at PG level at this juncture is preposterous. Lot of ground work has to be done in providing the prerequisites presented in the preceding sections. In the absence of these prerequisites it would be difficult and inadvisable for any institution of higher learning to venture upon starting LIS Courses at the P.G. level in Telugu.

REFERENCES

1. Raju, A.A.N.: 'Foreword' (In Glossary of Library and Information Science by Dr. P. Soma Raju, Visakhapatnam, The Author, 1992).
2. .... Literature on Library Science in Telugu. *Herald of Library Science*, V.10, 1970, pp.130-139.
3. .... State of Library Science Literature in Telugu (*In* Perspectives in Library and Information Science, V.2. Lucknow, Print House, 1982. pp.165-181.

14

Need for User Education Programmes to Research Scholars in Social Sciences

The phenomenal growth of universe of knowledge resulting in 'Information explosion' and inter-disciplinary approach to research during the past four decades generated new demands on the services provided by the Libraries and Information Centres in our country. The rapid strides our country made in various spheres of national endeavour since independence and the efforts that are being made to sustain this development and attain more significant results in social development added new dimensions to the services rendered by Libraries and Information centres.

GROWTH OF SOCIAL SCIENCES RESEARCH IN INDIA

Research in any discipline helps in its growth and ensures new developments. It broadens the frontiers of knowledge and helps the growth, development and enrichment of the discipline. This equally applies to the field of Social Sciences. After independence, social sciences have been on the march in our country. This is because of the increase in the number of universities in the country after independence. In 1950-51 there were only 18 universities and 700 colleges. At present there are 160 universities and 5,500 colleges.[1] Several Institutions, and other centres of higher learning and research in the field of social sciences have also been established in the country. The universities, institutions and colleges have taken interest for the development of Social Sciences, of course, with the active support of Union and State Governments.

The objective of planed development and launching and execution of six live year plans created an awareness and need for accelerated social science research which can help the formulation and successful implementation of five year plans. Universities and other Research Institutions concerned with social science Research received due support from the University Grants Commission (UGC). Planning Commission, Research Wings attached to various Ministries of Union and State Governments and other International Agencies and Institutions.

The major share of research in social sciences may be credited to the accounts of Post-graduate Departments of Social Sciences in the Universities and their affiliated colleges.

GROWTH IN M. PHIL/PH. D. ENROLMENT

In Indian universities M. Phil is the first research degree which is introduced after a Masters degree and which can be offered as a part of Ph.D. Programme. All the universities offer facilities for research in social Sciences for students as well as teachers leading to the award of M. Phil/Ph.D. degrees. Few universities still have the provision for research leading to Master of Literature (M. Litt). No statistics are available as to the number of scholars registered for research degrees in the universities every year in the field of social sciences. But the number is. increasing year after year. This can be inferred from the increased number of Ph.D. degrees awarded by the universities in India. In 1967 Indian universities awarded 1849 Ph.D.'s and this rose to 2717 in 1970.[2] In the year 1977-78, the universities in India awarded

1677 Ph.Ds and this rose to 2267 during the year 1981-82. A total of 9832 Ph. Ds were awarded by the universities in India between 1977-78 and 1981-82.[3] The enrolment for Ph. D. degrees was also steadily increased. In 1973-74 a total of 2275 candidates registered for Ph. D. and this rose to 2830 in 1976-77.[4]

THE SOUTH INDIAN SCENE

At present there are 35 universities and institutions deemed to be universities in South India. These universities have 203 Social Science Departments which offer M. Phil and Ph. D programmes in Social Sciences.[5] During the years 1977-1982 i.e. within a stream of live years a total number of 1942 candidates were enrolled for M. Phil programmes of which 766 candidates were awarded M. Phil degrees.[6]

Doctoral Research too in the South Indian universities gained momentum after independence. These universities awarded a bare twenty seven doctorates before 1950. After 1950 phenomenal increase was noticed in the number of Ph.Ds. The increase in the number of Ph.Ds during past three and half decades in shown in parenthesis beginning from 1951-60 (44), 1961-70 (172), 1971-SO (608) and 1981-84 (568). For 65 Ph. Ds information about the date of award was not available. During the years 1951 and 19X4 a total number of 1457 Ph. D. degrees were awarded by the universities. Thus Social Science Research in South Indian universities in terms of number of Ph. Ds has shown an impressive growth over the last three and half decades.[7] This growth rate is due to increase in the number of universities and colleges. Another important reason for phenomenal increase in the enrolment of Research Scholars in the mid-70's was due to the implementation of V-plan scales for teachers in Indian universities as well as affiliated and constituent colleges. The U.G.C. and State Governments initially insisted on all lecturers working in under-graduate and post-graduate colleges possessing a research degree of at least— M. Phil, in order to be eligible to receive the revised U.G.C. pay scales.

U.G.C. ASSISTANCE TO RESEARCH SCHOLARS

U.G.C. under its special research programmes such as College Humanities and Social Science Improvement Programme (COHSIP) and Faculty Improvement Programme (FIP) helping Research Scholars by way of scholarships/fellowships and the University Departments and colleges with handsome grants for the development of social science research.

The FIP Programme was introduced by the U.G.C. during the V-Plan and liberal giants were made to encourage working teachers to get paid leave to pursue research. This programme did help a number of teachers to work for M. Phil and Ph. D. who would not have done so without salary protection under the FIP Programme of the U.G.C. This assistance as well as other scholarship programmes of U.G.C. has also greatly contributed for the increase in the enrolment of research scholars in the Departments of Social Sciences in the Universities. The Research Scholars should be instructed in the use of library resources for deriving maximum benefit.

OBJECTIVES OF USER EDUCATION

The objective of user education is to furnish library users with some degree of familiarities with library and Information services and to impart knowledge and skills needed for identification and retrieval of relevant information. A.J. Evans et al identified the following educational and institutional objectives.[8]

1. To enable the individuals to do immediately after the instruction, tasks that they could not do well, if at all prior to instruction.
2. To secure change in behaviour or attitudes resulting from instruction and
3. To secure an embodiment of the skills as a fairly perma nent feature of work.

NEED FOR USER EDUCATION

The growth in the enrolment of research scholars in social

sciences for M. Phil/Ph. D degrees in the universities is a challenge and an opportunity for the university/college libraries in meeting the information needs of these research scholars. For effective use of the available literature, basic skills must be developed in the research scholars for which the librarians and teachers must take some responsibility.

The following factors will necessitate the introduction of User Education Programmes :

1. Majority of research scholars may he with the exce ption of teacher research scholars are new to research activity and have no idea of increasing volume of primary, secondary and tertiary sources of information in the social sciences.
2. The increased output of literature in various forms baffle the budding research scholars as to their scope, content and arrangement.
3. The research scholars mostly Masters' degree holders in any one of the social sciences without any pervious research experience and exposure to such varried sources of information, find it difficult at the initial stages to make a good beginning in their research endeavour.
4. Absence of proper guidance in bibliographic search may lead to ineffective literature search and may result in the wastage of time and energy of the research scholars. This may dampen the enthusiasm of the scholars for pursuing their endeavour.
5. There are instances where almost the same topic has been selected for research by more than one research scholar. This type of duplication of research can be avoided if the scholars arc properly guided to refer to necessary bibliographical tools for the selection of topics for research.

ROLE OF UNIVERSITY/COLLEGE LIBRARIES

The Laws of Library Science especially the second law "every reader his/her document" and the third law "every document its reader" clearly underline the need for libraries in helping the readers, in this context, the research scholars. The staff of the university/college libraries are belter placed for undertaking 'User Education' with the cooperation of the faculty concerned.

Course Contents and Methods of Instruction

With the cooperation of the Faculty of Social Sciences university library can design a short-term course of 3 to 5 days duration depending upon the needs of the research scholars. The said course may include :

1. *General Background*
    - 1.1 Value of Social Science Information
    - 1.2 Sources of Social Sciences Information
    - 1.3 Agencies concerned with Social Science Research in India and abroad
    - 1.4 Activities of ICSSR with special reference to National Social Science Documentation Centre (NSSDC).
2. *Keys to the use of the Library Resources*
    - 2.1 Library Classification
    - 2.2 Cataloguing and Indexing
    - 2.3 Bibliographical Tools
    - 2.4 Automated devices (if any).
3. *Literature search techniques*
4. *Practical Experience*
    - 4.1 Exposure to use of audiovisual equipment
    - 4.2 Methods of recording bibliographical references
    - 4.3 Instruction in the use of bibliographical and other reference tools
    - 4.4 Compilation of bibliographies.
5. *Evaluation and Feedback*
    - 5.1 Questionnaire method

5.2 Interview method

The course can be conducted through formal lectures, seminars and workshops by the effective use of audio-visual equipment. Visit to other library and Information Centres and Data Banks specialised in social sciences research collections and services will also help the research scholars.

UNESCO Guides

The two UNESCO guides 1. *Guidelines for the Organisation of training Courses*[9] and 2. *Education and Training of courses of scientific and technical information,*[10] will also be of immense help for Teachers and Information Specialists interested in organising user studies, seminars and workshops for education and training of users of social sciences information. These two can serve as basic tools for those organising user education programmes at the University level and intended to have particular application to circumstances in developing countries.

CONCLUSION

There is a pressing need for University/College Libraries to undertake User Education Programmes to enable the research scholars to utilize the library resources in most fruitful and beneficial manner. This will go a long way in bringing out qualitative change in Social Science Research in Indian Universities and Institutions of higher learning. The ICSSR through its Regional Centres, no doubt has been organising "Short Term Foundation Courses on Research Methods in Social Sciences". The Contents of this course include only one item on "Sources of Social Sciences Information" devoting one or two lectures. This may not serve the desired purpose. Some of the departments in the Faculty of Social Sciences in the Universities do conduct "Research Methodology Courses" to their M. Phil/Ph.D. Scholars. A study was conducted by J.M. Reddy and P. Satyanarayana as to the content and structure of Ph.D. Programmes in Social Sciences in South Indian Universities.[11] Another study was undertaken by B.A.V. Sharma and P. Satyanarayana as to the content and structure of M. Phil, programmes in Social Sciences in South Indian Universities.[12] These two studies did not reveal any programme or course or content in the syllabi for user education programmes to Research Scholars in Social Sciences.

Therefore it is sine-quo-non for the University Libraries in India to undertake user education programmes with the collaboration of Library & Information Science Departments to help research scholars for the optimum utilization of the existing library resources. The introduction of these programmes will certainly enhance dignity and prestige of university libraries and also bring due recognition and importance to our profession. The quality of research output will also be greatly enhanced.

REFERENCES

1. *University News,* V 25, N 25, Sept. 16, 1986. p.l.
2. Indian Council for Social Science Research (ICSSR), New Delhi. Doctorates in Social Sciences, Publication No. 20.
3. U.G.C., New Delhi, Report for the year 1982-83, p. 130.
4. U.G.C., New Delhi, University Development in India, Basic Facts & Figures, 1972-73-1976-77. Part-I, Section-C, 1981, p. 950.
5. Reddy, J.M. and Satyanarayana, P., Ph. D. Programmes in Social Science in South Indian Universities, Hyderabad ICSSR Southern Regional Centre, 1984, p. 36 (Mimeo graphed).
6. Sharma, B.A.V. and Satyanarayana, P. M. Phil Programmes in South Indian Universities, a study of Content and Structure, Hyderabad, ICSSR Southern Regional Centre, 1982. p. 32 (Mimeographed).
7. Reddy, J.M. and Satyanarayana, P. *op. cit.,* p. 37.
8. Evans, A.J., et al, Education and training of Users of Scientific and Technical Information ; UNISIST guide for teachers. Paris, UNESCO, 1977, p. 7.
9. Atherton, P, Guidelines for the organisation of training courses, workshops and seminars in scientific and technical information and documentation. Paris, UNESCO, 1975. 88p.
10. Evans, A.J. Et al ; *op. cit.,* 143p.
11. Reddy, J.M. and Satyanaryana, P. *op. cit,* 83p.
12. Sharma, B.A.V. and Satyanarayana, P, *op. cit.,* 56p.

Facet 5
LEGAL DEPOSIT

15

A Look into the Working of the Press and Registration of Books Act, 1867 in Andhra Pradesh

INTRODUCTION

In India the history of law relating to the Press and Books can be traced from the days of East India Company that paved the way for the British Colonial Rule in India. The advent of printing presses and publishing houses contributed the publication of books and other 'inflammatory material' on the colonial rule. Those in the fields of writing, publishing and printing gave thought to organize a system for keeping a record of publication. The East India Company was urged to keep a record of publications. A system of voluntary registration of publications was evolved but failed. Therefore, it was found necessary to establish a system of compulsory registration of published documents and prompted the authorities to enact laws to control and regulate the Press and

Publication activity in the Country. The earliest surviving enactment specifically directed against the Press and Publication activity was passed in 1867 the Press and Registration of Books Act, 1867 (Central Act 25 of 1867). This Act enabled the government to regulate the printing press and newspapers by a system of compulsory registration and to preserve copies of books and other material printed in India.

After independence Government of India enacted Delivery of Books and Newspapers (Public Libraries) Act, 1954 to provide free delivery of books and newspapers to the National Library, Kolkata and three designated public libraries in the country. These two acts have contributed the genesis and emergence of legal deposit in the country and helped to achieve some sort of bibliographical control of Indian Publications.

THE PRESS AND REGISTRATION OF BOOKS ACT, 1867

The Act, which was passed in the year 1867 by the British Colonial Rulers, was to regulate and control the printing presses and later newspapers and also for the preservation of copies of books and newspapers printed in India and their registration. The positive aspect of this Act was to preserve the intellectual output of the country for posterity. The negative aspect of the Act was to keep an eye on the intellectual awakening in the country, which may go against the interests of the colonial rulers. The Preamble of the Act states that "an Act for the regulation of printing presses and newspapers, for preservation of copies of books and newspapers published in India and for the registration of such books and newspapers".

OBJECTIVES

The main objectives of act are to — 1. Secure information from printing houses or establishments and their publications, 2. Preserve copies of every book and newspaper printed in India, 3. Regulate Printing Presses and Newspapers and 4. Prevent publication of anonymous literature.

PROVISIONS OF THE ACT

The Act contains seven parts as mentioned below:

1.	Part-I	Preliminary (Sections 1 and 2)
2.	Part-II	Of Printing Presses and Newspapers (Sections 3 to 8C)
3.	Part-III	Delivery of Books (Sections 9 to 11B)
4.	Part-IV	Penalties (Sections 12 to 17)
5.	Part-V	Registration of Books (Sections 18 and 19)
6.	Part-V-A	Registration of Newspapers (Sections 19A to 19L)
7.	Part/VI	Miscellaneous (Sections 20 - 23)

IMPORTANT PROVISIONS

The seven Parts of the Act consist forty-six sections covering various provisions of the Act. Some of the important provisions are briefly presented below:

DELIVERY OF PRINTED BOOKS AND NEWSPAPERS

Section 9 (Part-III) of the Act deals with the delivery of printed books as gratis to the government. This section stipulates that printed copies of the whole of every book which shall be printed in India together with all maps and prints, etc, be delivered by the Printer at such place and to such officer as the State Government shall by notification in the official gazette from time to time. The Printer has to deliver *three copies* of each publication free of expense to the State Government within a calendar year.

Likewise Section 16-A (Part-IV) of the Act stipulates that the Printer of every newspaper shall deliver at such place and to such officer as the State Government by notification in the official gazette direct and free expense to the government two copies of each issue of such newspaper as soon as it is published.

PENALTIES FOR NOT DELIVERING BOOKS AND NEWSPAPERS

Section 16 (Part-IV) of the act stipulates that if any printer of any book fails to deliver three copies of the book printed by him, he shall be fined not exceeding Rs.50/- (Rupees fifty) for each default by a Magistrate having jurisdiction in the place where the book was printed.

Likewise section 16-A (Part-IV) stipulates that if any printer of any newspaper published in India neglects to deliver the copies of the same, shall be punishable on conviction by a Magistrate having jurisdiction in the place where the newspaper is printed with a fine which may extend to Rs.50/- (Rupees fifty) for every default. These two provisions i.e. 16 and 16A are analogous to Sections 3 and 3A of Delivery of Books and Newspapers (Public Libraries) Act, 1954.

REGISTRATION OF BOOKS AND NEWSPAPERS

Section 18 (Part-IV) of the Act stipulates that such officer shall keep at such office and books so received as the State Government shall appoint for this purpose. The said officer has to maintain a catalogue of books printed in India wherein shall register a memorandum of each and every book received by it. The memorandum contains fourteen particulars. These included full bibliographical details of each book and in addition consist whether the book is printed or lithographed, the name and residence of the proprietor of the copyright or any portion of such copyright.

Section 19A (Part-VA) of the Act stipulates that a catalogue of registers of books shall be published at the end of each quarter in the official gazette and copy of the same has to be sent to the Central Government.

Section 19 B (Part-VA) of the Act states that the Press Registrar shall maintain in the prescribed manner a register of newspapers. The said register shall contain full details of every newspaper published in India. These details include: title, language, periodicity, name of the editor, printer, publisher, place of printing, average number of pages, average number of copies printed, retail selling price and names and addresses of owners of the newspaper. Section 19 G of (Part-VA) of the Act stipulates that the Press Registrar shall prepare an annual report containing summary of the information obtained by him during the previous year in respect of newspapers in India and giving an account of working of such newspapers and copies thereof shall be forwarded to the Central Government.

It may be pointed that this Act is a Central Act but implementation of provisions of the Act has been entrusted to the State Governments. As per the provisions of the Act only the printer is held responsible while the publisher is not touched.

WORKING OF THE ACT IN ANDHRA PRADESH

Andhra Pradesh is one of the leading States of Indian Union where a system of Public Libraries are functioning at different levels in the State right from the State Central Library as an apex library down to the village libraries and Book Deposit Centres. The system is a result of A. P. Public Libraries Act of 1960, which provides for a separate department of public libraries with director of Public Libraries as its administrative head.

As per section 20 (Part-VI) of the Act, Govt. of Andhra Pradesh have framed rules (Andhra Pradesh Press and Registration of Books Rules, 1960) vie GO Ms. No. 2104, Home (General-A) Department dated 10.10.1960. In GO Ms No.235 Home (General-A) Department dated 11.02.1976, Govt. of A. P., have changed the designation of "Registrar of Books" as "Registrar of Publications". In GO Ms. No. 286 Education, dated 27.03.1973, Govt. of A. P. directed that the Director of Public Libraries (DPL) shall be Ex-Officio Registrar of Publications so as to ensure proper implementation of the provisions of Act in the entire State of A.P. With the help of District Magistrates and the Commissioner of Police Hyderabad City, the Registrar of Publications is implementing the sections 9 (delivery of gratis copies), 10 (receipt of copies, 11 (disposal of copies), 11A (Copies of newspapers), 18 (registration of memoranda of books) and 19 (Publication of memoranda registered) i.e. the functions relating to "delivery of books" and registration of books".

Sections 3, 4, 5, 7, 8, 8-A, 8-B, 8-C, 12, 13, 14, 15, 15-A, 16, 16-A, 16-B and 17 are dealt with by the District Magistrates / Commissioners of Police. These sections deal with "starting of printing presses and newspapers" and "penalties".

RECEIPT OF PUBLICATIONS BY THE OFFICE OF THE REGISTRAR OF PUBLICATIONS

As per section 9 (Part-III) of the Act and as per the A. P. Press and Registration of Books Rules, 1960 framed by the Govt. of A. P., the Office of the Registrar of Publications receives *three copies* of every book printed within the state of A. P, (Rules 4 and 5). Similarly as section 11-A (Part-III) of the Act, the Office of the Registrar of Publications receives *two copies* of each issue of such newspaper. Out of three copies of all books received, one copy is deposited in the 'Reference Library' maintained by the Office of the Registrar of Publications, the second copy is deposited at State Central Library (SCL), Hyderabad and the remaining third copy is sent to Parliament Library, New Delhi. The two copies of each issue of newspaper(s) received at the Registrar's Office are preserved only for two years.

As per Section 19 (Part-V) of the Act and as per rule of the rules framed by Govt. of A. P. quarterly catalogues prepared on the basis of the receipt of books at the Office of the Registrar of Publications, should be published in the official gazette for the information of the public. But this is not being done due to administrative constraints.

CONSTRAINTS IN THE EFFECTIVE IMPLEMENTATION OF THE ACT

The Registrar of Publications, Govt. of A. P. has been facing some problems in the effective implementation of certain provisions of the Act and Rules framed by the Govt. of A. P. Rule 7 (a) states that "every keeper of printing press shall within ten *days* of the first day of January, the first day of April, the first day of

July and the first day of October each year forward to the concerned District Magistrate or if the Press is situated within the limits of twin cities of Hyderabad and Secunderabad, to the Commissioner of Police, Hyderabad a return in the 'format'.... of all the books printed at his press in the quarter immediately preceding the said dates, or if no books have been published at the Press, a statement to that effect".

The Rule 7 (b) states that "The Commissioner of Police and the District Magistrate shall send to the Registrar within 26 days after the close of each Quarter a consolidated quarterly return in Form-II.... all the books printed and issued from various printing processes within their respective jurisdictions during the quarter". This provision is not satisfactorily implemented.

The concerned District Magistrate / Commissioner of Police are not able to initiate proper action to get quarterly reports from the printing presses due to their pre-occupation with other important and pressing government business. In the present day government developmental activities getting quarterly reports from the printing presses gets least priority in the scheme of things of the government. The result is that the Registrar of Publications is not able to get quarterly list of publications to initiate action to get such of those publications from the printers as per the provisions of Act and Rules. The provisions of the Act is not implemented effectively mostly at the district level. The situation is somewhat better in Hyderabad Police Commissionerate, where sixty per cent (60%) of printing presses have been confirming to the provisions of the Act.

NEED FOR COOPERATION AND COORDINATION

For effective implementation of the Act, the cooperation and coordination of the Government Departments such as Home Department, Commercial Taxes, Municipal Administration, Panchayat Raj and the District Collectorates is very essential. The declaration submitted at the time of starting a new printing press to the District Magistrate / Commissioner of Police has to be regularly communicated to the Registrar of Publications so as to enable him to know the state of printing activity in the State and initiate necessary administrative measures to get the printed books, periodicals and newspapers from such printing presses.

NUMBER OF BOOKS RECEIVED

It has been estimated that since 1953 the Registrar of Publications has received over 50,000 books and these are maintained as Reference Collections. The Table (See Annexure) provides an idea of the number of printing presses at work in Andhra Pradesh and the number of newspapers, periodicals and books registered at the Office of the Registrar of Publications, Govt. of A. P., between the years 1998-99 and 2003-04.

The Office of the Registrar of Publications is maintaining a catalogue of these publications and the quarterly lists have to be published in the official gazette as per the provisions of the Act and Rules. This is not being done at present due to administrative difficulties such as lack of sufficient staff and infrastructure.

BOOK PURCHASE UNDER RRRLF SCHEME

The Rajah Ram Mohan Roy Library Foundation (RRRLF), Kolkata provides matching grant for the purchase of books every year to the respective State Governments. The Department of Public Libraries, Govt. of A. P. through Press Notification invites specimen copies of books from Publishers and Authors with the condition that "as per the Publication Act, in respect of books printed in Andhra Pradesh, 03 copies must be submitted to the Registrar of Publications... they should submit the xerox copy of the acknowledgement from the Registrar of Publications, Hyderabad or any other evidence to the effect that they have submitted 3 copies to the Registrar of Publications".

This condition insist the Publishers / Authors to submit three copies each publication to the Registrar of Publications if they wish to consider their publications for purchase under the said scheme along with one more copy for the said purpose. This condition indirectly compels the Publishers / Authors to conform to the provisions of the Act and the receipt of publications for registration at the Office of the Registrar of Publications, Govt. of A. P., is some what encouraging.

IMPLICATIONS TO LIBRARIANS

This Act has no direct bearing on the Librarians / Libraries, except those working at State Central Libraries (SCLs). Some ot the SCLs have been receiving a copy of the printed book under the provisions of the Act not directly from the Printer but from the assigned agency. In the case of Andhra Pradesh, it is the Registrar of Publications. The professionals working in these libraries must know the provisions of the Act and its role to achieve some sort of bibliographical control directly or indirectly of Indian Publications.

CONCLUSION

This Act is one of the earliest Acts enacted during the British Colonial Rule to have control over Printing Presses and Publications emanating from various parts of the country and which may go against the interests of the then British Rulers. After independence the Act has lost its sheen and many provisions have no direct relevance to present day needs. However, the Act continues to be in operation, which enables the government to know the state of affairs of printing presses and printed publications. The Act provides for some sort of 'control' over the printing presses, newspapers and periodicals. Experts feel that there is a common bond between the Press and Registration of Books Act (1867), Delivery of Books and Newspapers (Public Libraries) Act, 1954 and the Copyright Act (1967). They suggest steps for amalgamation of the provisions of the D. B. Act and P.R.B. Act to make implementation more efficient and less burdensome to the Printers, Authors and Publishers as the case may be.

Andhra Pradesh is one of the few states in the Country to have a separate Office of the Registrar of Publications to take charge of printed books and other publications received under the provisions of the Act. The Act is working satisfactorily though not vigorously due to administrative constraints and lack of support and cooperation from the implementing agencies. It appears that the working of the Act is far better in Andhra Pradesh than most of the States of the Indian Union.

16

The Delivery of Books and News Papers (Public Libraries) Act 1954 and National Bibliographical Control

INTRODUCTION

India with many languages including English as a language of administration, education and research emerged as one of the ten largest book producing countries of the World. According to Federation of Publishers and Book Sellers Association in India (FPBA) about 60,000 titles are published annually in the Country in all the major Indian Languages including English, which takes the lion's share[1]. To have bibliographic control over these publications at the national level requires two operations viz. *1. Production and publication of Current National Bibliography on a regular and continuous basis, and 2. Preparation of Retrospective Bibliographies.*

With a view to have bibliographical control over current

publications many countries the World over have enacted legal deposit legislation and established national bibliographical agencies to bring out Current National Bibliographies. UNESCO and IFLA have played a prominent role in the spread of the concept of Universal and National Bibliographical Control and assisted the member countries especially developing countries by providing expertise and material assistance as well to realize the concept of national bibliographical control.

GENESIS OF LEGAL DEPOSIT IN INDIA

Luhn defined legal deposit as "the requirement enforceable by law, to deposit with one or more specified agencies copies of publications of all kinds reproduced in any medium or with any process for public distribution, lease or sale"[2].

Legal deposit in India had its genesis with the passing of the delivery of Books and Newspapers (Public Libraries) Act, 1954 to institutionalize the system that helps the preservation of Country's cultural and intellectual heritage embodied in documents. The purpose of the Act is to ensure total coverage through compulsory deposit of a copy every publication published within the Country to the National Library at Kolkata and three designated depository libraries i.e. 1. *Connemera Public Library, Chennai, 2. Central Library, Mumbai,* and *3. Delhi Public Library, Delhi.*

This enabled the National Library and the three designated libraries to receive publications from the publishers free of cost and contributed to the emergency of legal deposit in our country.

GROWTH OF PUBLISHING INDUSTRY

Publishing Industry in the Country has gone a long way during the past five decades since the enactment of D. B. Act in 1954. Bandyopadhyay opines that "the publication industry has expanded enormously in terms of range or subjects covered and total number of titles appearing in these subjects. Publications in regional languages have risen in an increasing proportion, even as English remains the predominant language of publication in the country followed by Hindi. Also a widening range of quality publications is being brought out every year in the regional languages"[3].

RECEIPT OF BOOKS AT THE NATIONAL LIBRARY

It has been observed that the receipt of books at the National Library, Kolkata under D. B. Act, 1954 is not encouraging. The reason for this state of affairs is lack of cooperation from the publishers. It has been estimated that not more than 30% to 40% of publications published in the country are delivery to the National Library under D. B. Act, 1954. Mandal observes that "the reasons for non-submission of books are many. Some publishers especially the new in the trade are not aware of the obligations. It is estimated that the number of registered publishers exceeds 11,000. But most of them are medium or small concerns. It is observed that more than 50% of the total number belongs to individual publishing concerns. Not more than 10% or so are members of any organized associations or guild of publishers. This makes difficult for the National Library to get information about their publications and make them aware of the legal deposit. It is also observed that publishers do not find any incentive to submit a book because submission does not lead to increase in the sale of books"[4].

Another important reason for this state of affairs is the "seven book syndrome". It means that under the Press and Registration of Books Act, 1867 a Printer has to send three copies of each publication to the Registrar of Publications / Dept. of Information and Publications or any other designated office of the concerned State. In addition under the DB Act, 1954 every publisher has to send one copy to the National Library and a copy each to three designated libraries. The burden of sending seven copies of each publication by registered post to the concerned authority that too bearing the postal expenses by the Printer / Publishers is another discouraging factor. Therefore, the two acts i.e. P.R.B. Act, 1867 and D. B. Act 1954, is mostly implemented in breach.

NO. OF BOOKS RECEIVED AT THE NATIONAL LIBRARY

Abuzar states that "the highest number of publications received in a year in the National Library was 37,311 in the year 1956-57, the first year of the receipt after the amendment of the Act. But an analysis of the yearly receipt of books in the National Library under the Act reveals that, there was a gradual decrease in it. The average receipt of books in the library in 1950s was 26,000, in 1960s, it was 19,000, in 1970s, it was 18,000 and in 1980s it was 16,000.[5]

The receipt of books at the National Library, Kolkata for a five year period i.e. 1998-99 to 2002-03 is given blow:

Table-1

Year	1998-1999	1999-2000	2000-2001	2001-2002	2002 2003	Total
No. of Books Received	15,922	20,012	19,951	18,212	21.155	95,525

Source: National Library, Kolkata

According to Federation of Publishers and Book Sellers Association in India (FPBA) the annual book production in India is 60,000 titles. This may not be a correct figure. As many of the publishers especially Author / Individual Publishers are not members of this Association. If we consider 60,000 as a base figure and can be depended upon, the National Library receives one third of the total publications under D. B. Act, 1954. The receipt of books at the National Library does not reflect the actual situation obtaining in the country as to the number of books published annually. During the five-year period National Library, Kolkata received 92,252 books. On an average National Library received 18,450 books annually which is almost one third of the total books annually published in the Country as per the figure of 60,000 arrived at by the Federation of Indian Publishers and Book Sellers in India.

RECEIPT OF BOOKS BY THE DEPOSITORY LIBRARIES

As per the provisions of the D. B. Act, 1954 and rules made under thereof three libraries i.e. 1) State Central Library, Mumbai; 2) Connemera Public Library, Chennai, and 3) Delhi Public Library, Delhi, have been designated as Depository libraries to receive a copy of each of the publications emanating from the Country. The following Table provides figures pertaining tot he receipt of Publications during the five-year period i.e. 1998-99 - 2002-2003.

Table 2

Name of the Library	Year					Total
	1998-1999	1999-2000	2000-2001	2001-2002	2002 2003	
Connemera Public Library, Chennai	7,745	9,612	10,544	12,392	12,893	53,186
Central Library, Mumbai	7,840	10,653	12,671	12,511	12,537	56,212
Delhi Public Library, Delhi	12,338	10,525	12,511	13,383	12,487	61,244

Source, National Library, Kolkata

If we compare the figures provided for in Tables 1 and 2 it is evident that National Library, Kolkata has been receiving more number of books than the three designated Depository Libraries. Of the three depository libraries, Delhi Public Library has been receiving more books than the remaining two Depository Libraries at Chennai and Mumbai. During the five-year period Delhi Public Library received 61,244 books followed by State Central Library Mumbai 56,212 and Connemera Public Library, 53,186. On an average Connemera Public Library at Chennai, Central Library at Mumbai and Delhi Public Library, Delhi, received 10,637; 11,242 and 12,544 books respectively. Whereas the annual receipt of books on an average during the five-year period at National Library was 18,450. But even this higher receipt of books by the National Library than the three deposit Libraries is only one third of the total books published annually in the Country.

NATIONAL BIBLIOGRAPHICAL CONTROL

As stated already bibliographical control at the national level required two operations viz. 1) Production and Publication of Current National Bibliography on regular and continuous basis; and 2) Preparation Retrospective National Bibliographies.

One of the objectives of Central Reference Library, Kolkata was to publish National Bibliography for the Country. The enactment of D. B. Act, 1954 enabled National Library to receive books published in the Country under legal deposit. This gave impetus for bringing out India's National Bibliography. The first quarterly issue of Indian National Bibliography (INB) appeared on 15th August, 1958, the independence day of Country. The INB includes books in fifteen Indian languages received by the National Library. However, the publication of INB has its ups and downs. It was marred by erratic periodicity and discontinuity on few occasions. The coverage was also not satisfactory and does not reflect actual number of books published annually in the Country. As it has to depend upon the receipt of books at the National Library under D.B.Act, 1954, which is only one third of annual publications in the country, the comprehensive of coverage is blurred and effective bibliographical control of Indian publications is not fully achieved. A comparative table of annual receipt of books by the National Library and their inclusion in the INB for a five period is given below:

Table 3

Year	1998-1999	1999-2000	2000-2001	2001-2002	2002 2003
Books received by National Library	15,922	20,012	19,951	18,898	20,309
Inclusion in INB	9,163	12,486	12,725	9,752	9,448

Source: National Library and Central Reference Library

It is clearly evident from the above Table that out of the total books received by the National Library each year for five-year period about 35% to 50% of books are listed in the INB. The

National Library might not have accessioned all the publications it receives for various reasons and norms set by it for accessioning / non-accessioning certain publications. Likewise, Central Reference Library might have set out certain norms for inclusion / non-inclusion of certain documents in the INB. But the outcome is that INB is not able reflect the larger percentage of publications emanating from the Country. Abuzar opines that "Non-inclusion of 65% of the receipts suggests a stance of tedium to national bibliographical control program; hence no question of any efforts for supplementing the data from the receipts of other three libraries arose ever whatever may be the reason, the coverage in INB stands to be 15 to 20% of the total number of books produced in the Country"[6].

WORKING OF D. B. ACT, 1954

The D. B. act 1954 has been in operation for the past five decades. The objectives for which the act has been put on the statute book were not fully realized due to administrative problems, deficiencies in the act and non-cooperation from the publishers. The concept of legal deposit and national bibliographical control were not fully realized. The provisions of act were not fully enforceable due to very soft penal provisions against the defaulters. Whatever provisions of penalty provided for in the Act have rarely been applied. The prescribed procedure for launching proceeding for conviction of the offender is cumbersome. There is no proper machinery at the State / District levels to identify the newly published books and their submission to National Library and three designated libraries. Due to 'Seven Book Syndrome' as already mentioned elsewhere, many publishers / printers were deliberately not sending their publications free of cost to the depository libraries. Therefore, the annual receipt of books at the National Library and other three depository libraries is not encouraging. Due to organizational and administrative problems, the working of the Act was not satisfactory during the past five decades.

SUGGESTIONS FOR THE BETTER WORKING OF D. B. ACT, 1954

To improve the situation experts and professionals concerned with legal deposit and bibliographical control, publishing industry and library and information professionals have offered suggestions for better working of the act.

Some of the important suggestions are as follows:

1. Limiting the total number of publications to be delivered by the Printer / Publishers under P. R. B. Act, 1867 and D. B. Act, 1954 may be to a maximum of four to five.
2. Steps to be taken for the amalgamation of the provisions of D. B. Act, 1954 and P. R. B. act, 1867.
3. The scope of the term 'publication' may be widened in the context of D. B. Act, 1954 to include digital and other electronic version of reading materials. A. V. materials, music- cassettes, videocassettes should also come within the orbit of legal deposit.
4. The Penal clause under the D. B. Act, 1954, to be made more rigorous by increasing the fine for default to Rs. 1,000/ - or five times the cost of the book which ever is higher.
5. The publisher may be freed from the obligation of sending books to the deposit libraries at their expenses. The National Library should meet the postal expenses incurred by the publishers.
6. The procedure for trial of offence under D. B. Act, 1954 may be simplified and procedure of summary trial under CRPC may be adopted. There should also be provision for designating a number of officials to launch prosecution against defaulters.
7. Due publicity be given through mass media like Press, Radio and Television about the provisions of the Act and the obligation of the Publishers to deposit copies of their publications to the designated libraries to safeguard our country's documentary heritage to the present and future generations.

8. The publishers who are meticulously adhering to the provisions of D. B. Act, 1954 and sending their publications to the designated deposit libraries may be suitably honored during National Library Week or any other suitable occasion.

CONCLUSION

To achieve effective National Bibliographical Control, we need legal deposit and a comprehensive, effective and Current National Bibliography. Though not satisfactory, legal deposite in the Country has been achieved through D. B. act, 1954. The Act has to be revitalized to have satisfactory legal deposit and comprehensive national bibliographical control. The coverage and comprehensiveness of INB needs to be improved and brought out regularly without any let or hindrance. Successful working of D. B. Act, 1954, very much depends upon the cooperation of publishers, and especially author publishers, book sellers, LIS professionals, law implementing agencies, bureaucrats who are at the helm of affairs and above all the Department of Culture, Government of India, which is the apex body under which the National Library and Central Reference Library function.

REFERENCES

1. Malhotra, D. N. A Giant Slumber: the great saga of Indian Publishing. In D. N. Malhotra, ED 50 years of publishing in India. New Delhi, Federation of Publishers and Booksellers Association in India, 1998. p. 13.
2. Luhn, B. Guidelines for Legal Deposit. Paris, UNESCO, 1981. p.21.
3. Bandyopadhyay, A. R. The Delivery of Books Act, 1954: Suggestions for a Fresh Look, *In* National Bibliographical Control: Problems and Perspectives, *Ed.* by A. A. N. Raju and L. S. Ramaiah. New Delhi, Allied Publishers, 2003. p.35.
4. Mandal, S. National Library of India, |n Regional Seminar on delivery of Books and Newspapers (Public Libraires) Act, 1954.Jan 24, 2006. Seminar Papers. Kolkata, National Library, 2006. p14-15.
5. Abuzar, Syed. National Bibliographical Control and Legal Deposit in India: An overview. *In* Information Management in Knowledge Society. Kolkata, IASLIC, 2005. p.425.
6. Ibid, p.426.

17

The Indian Copyright Act and Its Implications in the Digital Era

INTRODUCTION

The advent of Knowledge Society replacing Agricultural and Industrial Societies has resulted in the emergence of new forms of property which was the result of human intellect and endeavor. The new form of intellectual property has come to play a vital role in the lives human beings. Intellectual property is broken down into two major branches viz. *Industrial and Copyright Law.* Industrial property encompasses patents, trade marks and industrial designs.

Copyright Law covers artistic, musical and literary works. The term "Intellectual Property" has been given official recognition by the international community with the establishment of World Intellectual Property Organization (WIPO), a specialized agency of the U.N.

According to WIPO, the 'Intellectual Property' shall include rights relating to:

1. Literary, artistic and scientific works;

2. Performances of performing artists, phonograms and broadcasts;
3. Inventions in all fields of human endeavor;
4. Scientific discoveries;
5. Industrial designs;
6. Trademarks, service marks and commercial names and designations; and
7. Protection against unfair competition.

DEFINITION AND MEANING OF COPYRIGHT

According to OED "the exclusive right given by law, for a certain term of years to an author, composer, etc. or his assignee to print, publish or sell copies of his original work".

Copyright is a unique kind of intellectual property and its importance is growing day by day after the emergence of knowledge societies in the developed as well as developing countries like India. It is the human beings who have the capacity of creativity. They can be authors, composers, artists and designers for creating and producing original works. It is they alone who have the exclusive rights to enjoy or they authorize others for certain acts in relation to: 1. Literary, dramatic, musical & artistic works, 2. Cinematograph film, and 3. Sound recordings. The basic areas that are covered under the copyright protection are in the domain of printing, music, communication, entertainment and computer industries.

SUBJECT MATTER OF COPYRIGHT PROTECTION

The copyright (Act) protects the works and other subject matter. For examples works like an original painting by Satish Gujral or M. F. Hussain, called an *artistic work* or a book by Pandit Jawharlal Nehru say *Discovery of India* or by Gurazada Appa Rao, Premchand, etc. called *literary work*, or a piece of music by Pandit Ravi Shankar, Bala Murali Krishna, or Pannalal Ghosh called *musical work* or 'Kanya Sulkam' staged at an auditorium called *dramatic work*. The other subject matters that can be copyrighted are called 'works' which include a film, a sound recording or a CD or a gramophone record, a broadcast on T.V. or Radio.

OBJECT OF THE COPYRIGHT ACT

The object of the Copyright Act is not only to protect the interests of the authors and artists but also enrichment of culture which is vital interest of each society and also protection of social interests. The Copyright Act has been enacted by several countries of the world to check piracy i.e. infringement of rights under the Act so that the fruits of labor put forth by the authors as copyright owners may be enjoyed by the deserving authors and copyright owners and not the pirates who indulge in plagiarism.

THE INDIAN SCENARIO

The earliest act relating to copyright was the Indian Copyright Act of 1847 enacted during the East India Company Rule. It was passed by the Governor General of India in the Council on 15th December 1847. This was followed by Indian Copyright Act of 1914, which was a modified version of British Copyright Act of 1911. The two Acts combining together constituted the copyright law in India. The Act of 1914 provided penalties for the infringement of the copyright, which was not considered as a criminal offence. The said Act authorized the destruction of infringed copies of their delivery.

After India's independence the technological, economic and social changes, which have taken place in the country necessitated a comprehensive copyright law. The result was the Copyright Act of 1957. This Act introduced several new features, which are as follows:

1. Establishment of Copyright Office under the control of Registrar of Copyrights who shall act under the directions of the Central Government.
2. Setting up of Copyright Board which will determine the reasonableness of rates of fees, charges or royalties claimed

by performing rights societies.

3. Definition of copyright was enlarged to include the exclusive right to communicate works by radio diffusion.
4. A cinematograph film will have separate copyright apart from its various components viz; story, music etc.
5. An author assigning copyright of his work is allowed the option to acquire the copyright after seven years with certain limitations.
6. The term of the copyright fixed to be the life of the author and a period of 25 years after his death.
7. A license may be issued to any library to make or cause to be made one copy of any book in which copyright subsists and which is not available for sale.
8. Provisions are made for regulating the activities of performing rights societies and also for controlling the fees, charges or royalties to be collected by them.
9. Certain rights akin to copyright are conferred on broadcasting authorities in respect to programs broadcast by them.
10. International copyright relations which are based on International treaties shall be regulated by specific orders to be made by Govt. of India.

AMENDMENTS TO THE COPYRIGHT ACT, 1957

The basic features of Indian Copyright Act 1957 conform to the provisions of the two International acts viz: 1. Berne Convention and 2. Universal Copyright Convention. India is member of both the conventions, which were revised at Paris in 1971.

The Indian Copyright Act was amended so far four times in the years 1983, 1984, 1994 and 1999 to keep pace with the changing times and requirements of the emerging knowledge society. The 1983 amendment provides for: a) provisions for compulsory licenses for translation and reproduction of foreign works required for instructional purposes, b) providing adequate protection to authors rights and c) removing administrative bottlenecks for administering the Copyright Act of 1957.

As the piracy of the word, sound recordings and cinematograph films increased to unimaginable proportions all the countries enacted stringent laws to curb the menace. India also initiated action in this direction. The 1984 amendment contained the following: 1) Increase the punishment provided for the infringement or violation of the copyright to three years with a minimum of six months and fine up to Rs.2 lakhs with a minimum of Rs. 50000. 2) Provision for the declaration of the offence of infringement of copyright as an economic offence and 3) To make provisions of the act applicable to video films and computer programs.

As the anti piracy provisions incorporated in 1984 amendment could not work effectively Govt. of India appointed a Working Group in 1987 to recommend suitable amendments taking into account the rapid advances made in Information and Communication technologies. As a result of the suggestions of the Working Group and the recommendations of the Joint Committee of the both the houses of the parliament, the copyright act was amended again in 1994. This amendment provides for: 1) Performers rights protection covering any visual or artistic presentation made live by one or more performers, 2) Copyright Societies seeking to promote collective administration of rights of authors, composers and other creative artists, 3) Assignment of copyright by an author or an artist to protect the interests of both the assigner and assignee and 4) Computer programs, cinematograph and films and sound recording protection.

The Copyright Act was again amended in the year 1999 which incorporated: 1) Amended definition of literary works, 2) Meaning of copyright in respect of computer program, 3) Increased term of copyright of performers from 25 years to 50 years, 4) New provisions pertaining to power of Govt. of India to apply the provisions relating to Broadcasting Organizations and performance to Broadcasting Organizations.

OTHER IMPORTANT PROVISIONS OF THE ACT

Chapter-IV of the Indian Copyright Act provides for rights of owners of copyright some of which include - right of assignment, mode of assignment, right of author to relinquish copy right, broadcast reproduction rights, performers' rights, special rights of authors and right to sue infringement.

Chapter-V of the Act provides for term of copyright some of which include-term of copyright in published literary, dramatic, musical and artistic works, anonymous and pseudonymous works, posthumous works, photographs, cinematograph film, sound recordings, Govt. works and works of International Organizations.

Chapter-II of the Act provides for three important authorities and institutions viz. 1) Copyright Office, 2) Copyright Board and 3) Copyright Societies.

Chapter-XI of the Act deals with infringement of the Act. This section deals with aspects such as: What is infringement? Common forms of infringement, principles of deciding infringement of copyright, factors involved in determination of infringement, special provisions in relation to sound recordings and video films and importation of infringing copies. Section 52 deals with acts not to be infringement of copyright.

Chapter-XII of the Act deals with three types of remedies for the violation of the copyright. These are: 1) Civil remedies, 2) Criminal remedies and 3) Administrative remedies.

IMPLICATIONS TO LICs

The Indian Copyright Act protects the authors of their intellectual property rights. At present reprographic service has become a common readers' service in most of our Libraries and Information Centers (LICs). Especially in Academic, Special and Research Libraries to meet the demands of the user community chapter/s from books, reports, reference books and from many other sources of information and sometimes the entire document from cover to cover is photocopied and made available to the user community. This is a clear violation of the Indian Copyright Act. As per the provisions of the Act license has to be obtained from the concerned authority for making photocopies available to the user community in case the concerned document is not available for sale. This provision applies only to rare and out of print documents and the period of copyright has not expired or lapsed.

There are instances where some of the Publishing / Bookselling Agencies without proper permission / authority sold photocopied editions of Universal Decimal Classification (UDC) and Dewey Decimal Classification (DDC) schedules at throw away prices. The same fate struck Colon Classification (CC) also. Many of the Library Schools have resorted to the same unethical methods to augment the schedules of classification for teaching practicals to a large number of students.

These unauthorized practices is a clear violation of Indian Copyright Act and liable for punishment under the relevant sections of the Act. It is the sacred duty of the library profession to protect and safeguard the intellectual property rights of authors, composers, artists and designers.

DIGITAL ERA AND THE COPYRIGHT

The advent of digital era made possible easy access to knowledge / information to the needy. Along with it we find violation of the provisions of the Copyright Act. Quite often we read in the newspapers plagiarism scandals of print and non-print media. The market is flooded with pirated editions of books, VCDs, films and other forms of non-print material causing financial losses to authors / copyright holders.

The classic example is Google's programme of creating searchable digital copies of the contents of university libraries. Three authors viz; Daniel Hoffman, Betty Miles and Herbert Mitgang have filed suit against Google's Print Library Programme - 'a searchable library of all world's printed books' - contending that said programme constituted "massive copyright infringement". But Google took shelter under 'Fair Use" provision of the copyright law.

This is just one example of violation of provisions of the Copyright Law in the digital environment. The Indian Copyright Act comes to the rescue of Copyright holder under such circumstances. For India and other developing countries rich in creative traditions including in music and films effective protection of copyright will be possible only if people are educated that piracy of intellectual property is no less criminal and anti-social than other kinds of theft. The enforcement agencies also should be vigilant of copyright violations and the violators should be severely dealt with as per the provisions of the Copyright Act.

REFERENCES

1. The Copyright Act (India), 1957.
2. Reddy, G. B. Intellectual Property Rights and the Law. Hyderabad, Gogia Law Agency, 2000.
3. Raju, A.A.N. The Indian Copyright Act and its implications to Libraries and Information Centres. In Satarkar, S.P., Ed. Intellectual Property Right and Copyright. New Delhi, Ess Ess Publications, 2003. pp.8-12.
4. Satarkar, S.P. Ed.: Intellectual Property Rights and Copyright. New Delhi, Ess Ess Publications, 2003.

Facet 6
OTHER ASPECTS

18

Bibliographic Organisation and Control in Social Sciences

SCOPE AND GROWTH OF SOCIAL SCIENCE LITERATURE

Social Scientists intending to make an original contribution to the growth of knowledge in their specified fields tend to build upon previous research. It is necessary for them to find out whether relevant research has already been carried out so as to provide a point of departure for new search and to avoid duplication of effort, wastage of time and resources. This can be possible on the availability of an effective bibliographic organisation and control of social science literature. The scope of Social Sciences is vast and varied. The *New Encyclopedia Britannica*[1] included the following subjects which deal with human behaviour in its social and cultural aspects under the category of Social Science viz : Economics, Political Science, Sociology, Social and Cultural Anthropology, Social Psychology and Social and Economic Geography and those areas of Education that deal with the social contexts of learning and the relation of the school to the social order. History is also regarded as one of the Social Sciences. Some would like to include all those subjects in the category of Social Sciences which deal with one or other aspects of society, others insist on the approach and methodology employed for the investigation of phenomena in question. ERA Saligman[2] defined Social Sciences as "those mental or cultural sciences which deal with activities of the individual as a member of a group ". He further categorised Social Sciences into three classes viz : the purely social sciences, the semi social sciences and the sciences with social implications. Yogesh Atal[3] identified the disciplines which come under the purview of social sciences in the ' Indian context' as those disciplines which receive support for research from the Indian Council for Social Science Research (ICSSR). These disciplines are : Economics, Commerce, Education, Management, Business Administration, Political Science, International Relations, Psychology, Public Administration, Sociology, Criminology and Social Work. ICSSR also gives support to research on 'Social Science ' aspects of the disciplines of Anthropology, Demography, Geography, History, Law and Linguistics.

The various subjects listed above under the purview of Social Sciences are gaining considerable importance and significance since the turn of the century because of tremendous advances human society has made in the field of Science, Technology and Scholarship. These advances definitely shrunk the world in the matter of distances amongst human societies both in developed and developing countries bringing in a new awareness and the necessity of study in depth of the social sciences. With frequent' explosions ' in the realm of knowledge one way to understand the growth of social sciences is to measure the output of literature in these disciplines and to properly organise the literature and disseminate the same in a most effective manner. The rapid growth in social sciences resulted in the torrent of published material which poses a constant problem to the Bibliographers, Documentalists as well as the Social Scientists, because of their different fused aspects and the variety of formats in which both macro and micro literature pours out incessantly.

BIBLIOGRAPHIC ORGANISATION AND CONTROL

Tremendous production of literature and data in all its forms and the multiplicity of information bewilder even active research workers. In the maze of information the bibliographer and the social scientist have to fight their way to discover a few useful bits of relevance which are extremely hard to extract as they are often repetitive. But Social Scientists and Bibliographers have taken a cue from natural scientists and have adopted their bibliographical techniques in organising, storing and the retrieval of social science information. This technique is currently known as 'Bibliographic Organisation'. V. W. Clapp defined bibliographic organisation "as the pattern of effective arrangement which results from the systematic listing of the records of human communication"[3]. This implies that the records of human communication of all kinds whether they are written or in the printed form should be effectively arranged so that they may serve some definite purpose. Bibliographic Organisation is not much different from bibliographic control since the latter has also been defined by UNESCO-Library of Congress Survey[5] as the "mastery over written and published records which is provided by and for the purpose of Bibliography ".

The spontaneous growth in the number of documents in a variety of forms, the complexity of subjects, the increase in the number of research workers and specialists and the complexity of approach towards documents in social sciences are the main factors which bring out the need for systematic bibliographic organisation. According to D. J. Foskett[6] the bibliographic organisation and control process consists of four main stages viz :1 Identifying the exact subject of research, 2. Locating the subject in a guide, 3. Locating the documents and 4. Locating the required information in the documents.

BIBLIOGRAPHIC TOOLS

In order to have effective bibliographic organisation and control, Library Scientists with the help of Social Scientists have developed effective bibliographic tools so as to meet the information needs of Social Scientists. To make known the existence of different types of documents, numerous bibliographical or secondary services have emerged which have in the discharge of their functions, produced Indexes, Bibliographies, Current awareness services, forth coming publication lists, Periodical lists, news summaries, Translation and Reprographic services etc. These services have done well in meeting the research needs of the social scientists. C. M. White made a comprehensive survey[7] of information and bibliographical services in the social sciences. A good number of reference works have come out under the Butterworths series, ' Information Sources for Research and Development' in which social sciences have been given due place. Norman Roberts has edited a book for social scientists[8].

It is not possible, for want of space, to discuss or list out other innumerable bibliographical tools produced from a large number of Libraries, Research Institutes, Societies and Commercial Organisations. Besides this, a number of libraries bring out printed catalogues which also serve as important tools for the identification and exploitation of social science literature. Some of the important components of the bibliographical systems are briefly discussed here.

NATIONAL AND TRADE BIBLIOGRAPHIES

National Bibliographies provide authoritative statements about the existence of documents and indicate the level and direction of publishing activity both in general and special areas. In UK, the British Library Bibliographic Service Division published *British National Bibliography* (BNB) a weekly list in classified order with Author and Title Indexes. The weekly list is supported by monthly, quarterly, annual and multi annual cumulations simplifying the problem of retrospective searching. Full bibliographical details are given for each document. BNB with its comprehensiveness serves as a bibliographical tool of great versatility. It may be used to answer many types of questions. Most of the Academic, Public and Research Libraries acquire a range of national bibliographies and display in their reference sections to meet ever growing needs of their clientele. Examples of other national bibliographies are *Bibliographic de la France* (France), *Canadiana* (Canada), *Deutsche Bibliographic* (Federal Republic of Germany), *National Union Catalogue* or the *Cumulative Book Index* (USA) and lastly but not least *Indian National Bibliography* (INB) which started publication in 1957 by the Central Reference Library, Calcutta. This has been modeled on the lines of BNB. In addition to the National Bibliographies few trade bibliographies also assist the searcher in the identification of current publications in a particular discipline. Examples of trade bibliographies are : *British Books in Print, Books in Print,* (Bowker). *Cumulative Book Index* (Whitaker), *Publishers Trade list Annual.* These current and other retrospective bibliographies assist in obtaining full bibliographical details of a published document.

Subject Bibliographies

National bibliographies list the publications of a given geographical area and the coverage is easily and clearly defined. Subject bibliographies on the other hand are numerous and varied. These bibliographies are prepared and published by numerous agencies and for different purposes and to widely different standards. In this paragraph attention will be concentrated on three examples of general level bibliographies in the social sciences. *The American Behavioural Scientist : Guide to recent publications in the social and behavioural sciences* (1965-) published by American Behavioural Scientist is an annual bibliography cumulates from a regular bi-monthly new publications section of the journal *American Behavioural Scientist* which also serves as a method of updating the annual volume. This is an example of a current awareness bibliography. The

International Bibliography of Social Sciences represents another type of bibliographical contribution. This work is prepared by International Committee for Social Science Information and Documentation and appears annually in four parts viz : *Sociology* (1951), *Political Science* (1952), *Economics* (1952) and *Social and Cultural Anthropology* (1955). Entries for the four volumes are culled from the publication programmes of many countries and also include periodical articles selected from nearly 2000 journals. Many other subject bibliographies are confined to a particular geographical area. Mention may be made of *Asian Social Science Bibliography* (Vikas, New Delhi) edited by N. K. Goil at the Institute of Economic Growth, Delhi. This classified bibliography in which most of the entries are either annotated or have abstracts is a useful tool to literature exploitation in the field. Bibliographers and Social Scientists must have the knowledge of existing bibliographies. If the literature search is in the nature of identification of existing bibliographies, the answer lies in the bibliographies of bibliographies. In this area one must cite T. Besterman,s *World Bibliography of Bibliographies,* 4th edn (Societa Bibliographica, Lausanne, 1965-66). It is a giant among bibliographical enterprise?. The work in five volumes lists over 117000 separately publised bibliographies arranged under 16000 subject headings which included many entries for social sciences. Another important serial bibliography is *Serial Bibliographies in the Humanities and Social Sciences* compiled by R. A. Gray Ann Arbor, Michigan, Pierian, 1969. For the location and identification of current bibliographies *Bibliographic Index* (1937-) (H W Wilson, New York) is a useful tool. This Index issued three times a year with annual cumulations lists bibliographies published separately or appearing as parts of a Books, Pamphlets and Periodicals. A full picture of previous efforts in the production of bibliographies of all types can be had in *Sources of Information in the Social Sciences* by C M White Edn 2, ALA, 1973. W A Katz[9] has made a detailed study and critical evaluation of these bibliographies.

PERIODICAL LISTS AND UNION CATALOGUES

Periodical literature provides nascent micro thought which is essential for research in any discipline. Literature for research purposes must necessarily concentrate upon journal or periodical literature which has assumed an important position in social science research. To assist the researcher in identification of the journals that are being published in a particular subject area or to ascertain other details such as periodicity, coverage, subscription etc. of a particular journal, periodical lists are being published to exploit this form of information. A bewildering array of means for the bibliographic control of periodicals has developed in the past twenty years. Davinson[10] discusses this aspect including bibliographies of periodicals and guides to contents of periodicals. The most useful general source for establishing the existence of journals in specific fields is *Ulrichs International 'Periodical Directory*, 17th Edn. (1977) (Bowker) which is a biennial publication listing over 55,000 periodicals by subject and title. This is a good example of bibliographical tools attempted on an international scale. There are other periodical lists which are on a smaller national scale. D. P. Wood Worth's *Guide to Current British Journals* (Library Association 1973) lists journals by their main subject interest. For India the *Guide to Indian Periodicals* (Rajasthan University, Jaipur) and *Press in India* published annually by the Registrar of News papers, Government of India are two important sources to know Indian Social Science Periodicals. The *International Social Science Journal* acts as an important tool to keep track of new journals in the social sciences. This quarterly publishes annually a list of new periodicals received at the UNESCO Social Science Documentation Centre. The *World list of Social Science Periodicals* 4th rev. & enlarged Edn (UNESCO, 1978) is another important tool in the field.

Local availability of a particular periodical cannot be taken for granted. When the required journal is not available it must be located elsewhere and made available to the researcher. Librarians have developed an efficient system to meet such demands by inter library lending. For effective functioning of an inter-library lending system the library profession has developed a tool known as 'Union Catalogues ' which indicate who has what. Mention may be made of a few outstanding Union Catalogues. *The 'National Union Catalogue* (USA), The *British Union-Catalogue of Periodicals* (Butter Worths, 1955-1957) which is a record of the periodicals in the British libraries, *Union list of Serials in Libraries of United States and Canada.*, 3rd edn (Wilson, 1965) which covers the period up to 1950 in five volumes. This work was extended to cover the decade 1950-1960 in two volumes as *New Serial Titles* 1950-60 : *Supplement to the union list of serials.* For India, ICSSR, New Delhi has brought out a number of union catalogues *of* social science serials for different states of the Indian Union with supplements. It has also brought out *Retrospective Cummulative Index of Indian Social Science Periodicals* (1976) which help the social scientist to find out the availability of periodicals in Indian Libraries.

LIBRARIES AND INSTITUTIONS CATALOGUES

Catalogues list the documents possessed by a library or an institution but where as bibliography lists documents according to determined characteristics without regard for institutional limitations, the catalogues of great libraries possess extensive social science collections. The British Museum libraries *General Catalogue of Printed Books to* 1955 (British Museum 1965) in 263 volumes with updating supplements is an important source for world social science literature. This catalogue has been updated by the publication of *Fife-year Supplements,* 1966-1970 (British Museum, 1971). Perhaps the most useful catalogue produced by the Library of Congress from research point of view is the *Library of Congress Catalog : Books: Subjects* which appears in quarterly issues with annual and multiyear cumulations. The companion series is the *National Union Catalogue : a cumulative Author List* which appears even more frequently. It is published on a monthly basis with quarterly, annual and multi-annual cumulations. This catalogue lists holdings of a number of important libraries in the

U.S. in addition to those of the Library of Congress. Many of the National Libraries also publish their catalogues. Publication of these catalogues which facilitate access to information is not confined to libraries only. Institutions and organisations with a strong interest in social sciences also bring out lists to make known their contributions to bibliographic organisation. For example the *Bibliography of Publications Issued by UNESCO or under its Auspices,* 1946-1971 (UNESCO, 1973) lists over 5000 published documents arranged by subject. Most of the titles listed fall under social sciences. Many specialist organisations through their libraries or Information Centres bring out catalogues which may be of immense use to social scientists. The Dag Hammarskjold Library of United Nations publishes 22 times a year *Current Bibliographical Information* which is a classified list. Many of the topics listed are of interest to social scientists. UNESCO also brings out a more useful up to date directory entitled *World Index of Social Science Institutions.* This directory provides systematic data on all those social science research, advanced training and documentation institutions and professional bodies for which information was available in the UNESCO Social Science Documentation Centre. Another outstanding tool for access to scholarly information in social sciences is the *London Bibliography of the Social Sciences* which began publication in 1931. This catalogue lists the holdings of the British Library of Political and Economic Science. The latest catalogue to be published from this library in 1973, is the 7th supplement for the period from 1969-1972 in 28 volumes.

NEWS INDEXES & SUMMARIES

News papers provide a mine of information on contemporary social, political, economic, educational and cultural events to (social scientists. Proper bibliographical organisation is essential to locate and identify any piece of information. Efforts have been made in this direction to produce Indexes to news paper articles, news items and other data. Some news paper publishers and commercial organisations have been publishing these Indexes.

Mention may be made of : *The Times Index* (1960)— appears quarterly with entries arranged alphabetically by subject, the *New York Times Index* (1913—) with annual cumulations, *Index to Pravada* (M) (1975—) by the American Association for the Advancement of Slavic Studies with annual cumulations, *Times of India Annual Index* another important tool for gaining access to the contents of a major Indian news paper, *Indian News Index, British Humanities Index* (1962—) is another important reference tool.

The commercial services which bring News Summaries, digest information gathered from a variety of sources including news papers. The best known of these are : *Keesigns' Contemporary Archives : Weekly Diary of Important World Events with Index Continually Kept up-to-date* (1931—) *African Recorder : a Fortnightly Digest of African Events* (1962—), *Asian Recorder : a weekly Digest of Asian Events* (1955—), *Africa Diary : Weekly Record of Events in Africa with Index* (1961—), *Facts on File : The Index of World Events* (1940—), *Data India.* These English language services provide valuable assistance as bibliographical tools.

DISSERTATIONS, THESES AND RESEARCH REPORTS

Dissertations and theses submitted to various universities and institutions of advanced learning constitute invaluable information sources to social scientists. The degree awarding institutions communicate knowledge about such research to the scholarly world through a list in some manner. These listings are published separately or shown in the annual reports with summaries some times. Effective bibliographic control is achieved through the publication of Indexes and Abstracts. Examples of such reference tool are : *Index to theses Accepted for Higher Degrees by the Universities of Great Britain and Ireland and the Council of National Academic Awards* (A) (ASLIB), which is arranged in broad subject categories, *Bibliography of Doctoral Dissertations accepted by Indian Universities* 1857-1970 published by Inter University Board of India and Ceylon, *Union List of Theses for Australia* published by University of Tasmania, *Union List of Theses for New Zealand* published by Newzealand Library Association, *Dissertation Abstracts International* (1938-). *Humanities and Social Sciences* Ann Arbor, Michigan Xerox University Micro films, which is a monthly Index provides abstracts of doctoral dissertations submitted to 345 Academic Institutions in the USA and Canada, *Research Abstracts* (ICSSR, New Delhi) which provides information on the findings of the research projects sponsored by ICSSR.

In recent years a greater amount of Social Science research is sponsored by a variety of agencies both national and international. In UK the main funding agency is Social Science Research Council. All the current and recently completed research supported by the Council is reported in its annual publication *Research Supported by the Social Science Research Council.* For a comprehensive view of social science research in UK the annual *Scientific Research in British Universities and Colleges,* V3 : *Social Sciences* (HMSO) is an important tool. The progress of research in Social Sciences in India is disseminated by ICSSR through its *News Letter* (1970—).

INDEXING & ABSTRACTING BULLETINS

These are most important tools for both current and retrospective searches. These help the Documentalist and the Social Scientist to locate and identify nascent information on any aspect of social sciences. A large number of such tools either covering the whole gamut of social sciences or of a particular branch is be ing published. Some of the outstanding Indexing and abstracting services covering a wide range of material in Social Sciences are : *Public Information Service Bulletin* (PAIS), *Social Sciences Index, Readers Guide to Periodical Literature, British Humanities Index* which covers nearly 400 British journals in the humanities and social sciences, *International Bibliography of Social Science* in four annual series in Economics, Sociology, Anthropology and Political

Science, *Australian Public Affairs Information Service* (APAIS) *Index India*, one of the most comprehensive Indexing bulletins being brought out by the University of Rajasthan, Jaipur, *Guide to Indian Periodical Literature*, a commercial venture.

In addition to these Indexing and abstracting services covering the whole field of social sciences, numerous other services exist in different areas of social sciences. Of these mention may be made of : *Sociological Abstracts, International Political Science Abstracts, Indian Public Administration Abstracts, Abstracts in Anthropology, Contents of Recent Economic Journals, Journal of Economic Abstracts, international Bibliography of Economics, Psychological Abstracts, Contents pages in Management, Current Management Literature, Top Management Abstracts British Eduction Index,' Sociology of Education Abstracts, Indian Education Abstracts, Higher Education Current Awareness Bulletin, Abstracts on Criminology and Penology, Index to Legal Periodicals, Geographical Abstracts, Urban Abstracts.* These are some of the important Indexing and abstracting services. R. A. Gray[11] listed 1400 Bibliographical Services. National lending library (UK) has done a systematic listing of available English language Indexing and abstracting services[13].

An interesting variation of the conventionally produced Indexing and Abstracting Bulletins is that of 'Gitation Index' devised by Egene Gardiedl fo the Institute of Scientific Information Philadelphia[13]. This is a computer produced Index in which the history of a particular paper is traced through its citation by subsequent authors. The *Social Science Citation Index* produced by Garfield has been found effective for tracing work following up particular lines of thought associated with known authors. It consists of the citation index, arranged alphabetically by author, a useful corporate Index of the authors' affiliations, a source Index of the original authors and a permuted subject Index. The same Institute also produces *Current Contents : Social Behavioral Sciences* giving copies of the contents pages of current periodicals week *by* week.

OTHER TOOLS

In addition to the preceeding conventional bibliographical tools social scientists are frequently exposed to various micro forms which are challenging the very existence of paper-based forms. The main reasons are economic considerations as the costs of conventional forms of publishing are touching the sky. There are certain cost advantages in publishing certain types of works in micro forms. Many out-of-print works are being published in micro film, micro card or micro-fiche. A number of specialist micro form publishing houses have been established whose publication programmes are of interest to social scientists. A few examples under this category are : *Middle East Datafile* (1975—-) by University Micro films, *Comprehensive Dissertation Index,* 1861-1972, 37 vols available in 800 micro fiches, *International Micro forms in Print* 1974-75 (Mansell, 1974), *Subject Guide to Micro Forms in Print* (Micro Card Editions, Washington).

Conferences, Seminars and Meetings are some of the important channels of communication which the social scientist generally attends for interaction with other social scientists. It is rather difficult to keep track of numerous national and international conferences and therefore requires some type of publication which lists past and forth coming events. An important tool which provides information about International meetings is *World Meetings : Social Behavioural Sciences, education and Management* published by World Meetings Information Centre Inc. Chestnut Hill, Mass (USA). Another important tool under this category is *BLL Conference Index* 1964-73 published by British Library lending Division , 1974, which lists 46,500 conferences under subject. This is updated by a monthly *Index of conference Proceedings Received by BLL.*

CONCLUSION

In the foregoing paragraphs an attempt has been made to give a birds eye view of the tools available for obtaining Bibliographic Organisation and Control in Social Sciences. The array of bibliographic activities found in USA, UK, Canada and even India has been vigorous and is assuming new dimentions. By and large, with varying degree of emphasis these bibliographical tools have been meeting the needs of researchers and specialists, as an effective mechanism for retrieval of Information. The concept of universal availability of publications and photo copying facilities including translation services needs to be strengthened. This can be possible with full cooperation and understanding between countries and inter-governmental organisations to make use of the vast amount of literature in social sciences in all the countries . and especially in the developing ones. A step in this direction was the launching of DEVISIS[14] (Development Science, Information System) an inter-governmental cooperative information system for social sciences sponsored by International Development Research Council (Canada), Organisation for Economic Cooepra-tion and Development (OECD) and UNESCO. Another landmark in organising information systems in social sciences at the international level is to extend the UNESCO's UNISIST[15] Inter-governmental Programme for Cooperation in the field of Scientific and Technological Information) programme to social sciences. This decision was taken at UNESCO's 18th general conference held in 1974.

REFERENCES

1. The *New Encyclopedia Britannica.* V16. Chicago Encyclopedia Britannica, Inc, 1974. 1980.
2. SALIGMAN, ERA. "What are the Social Sciences " *In Encyclopedia of Social Sciences.* VI. New York, MacMillan, 1959. P3).
3. ATAL, Y. "Social Sciences -India " *In Social Sciences in Asia* ed by Yogesh Atal. New Delhi; Abhinav Publications, 1974. 112.
4. CLAPP, V. W. "Bibliographic Organisation" *In* SHERA, JH and EGAN, M, Eds. *Bibliographic Organisation.* Chicago. The University of Chicago Press, 1950 p. 4.
5. UNESCO AND LIBRARY OF CONGRESS BIBLIOGRAPHICAL SURVEY. *Bibliographical Services; their present state and possibilities of improvement.* Washington. 1950 1.

6. FOSKETT, DJ. *Classification and Indexing in the Social Sciences* Edn2-London; Butterworths, 1974 p. 6.
7. WHITE, CM *et al.* Sources of Information in the Social Sciences. New Jersey; Bedminister Press, 1964.
8. ROBERTS, N. *Use of Social Science Literature.* London; Butterworths, 1977.
9. KATZ, WA. *Introduction to Reference Work, VI. Basic Information Source.* Edn3. New York; McGraw Hill, 1978 pp. 55—93.
10. DAVINSON, D. *The Periodicals Collection.* Edn2. London; Andre Deutsch, 1978 pp. 79 — 149.
11. GRAY, RA. *Serial Bibliographies in the Humanities and Social Science* Ann- Arbor, Michigan, Pierian Press, 1969.
12. NATIONAL LENDING LIBRARY (UK). *KWIC Index to English Language Abstracting and Indexing Publications being received by the National Lending Library.* Edn4. 1972.
13. LAZEROW, S. "Institute for Scientific Information " *In Encyclopedia of Library and Information Science.* V 12. New York; Marcel Dekker, 1974. 89—97.
14. *DEVSIS; The Preliminary design of an International Information System for Development Sciences.* Ottawa; IRDC Centre, 1976.
15. ATHERTON, P. *Hand Book of Information Systems and Services.* Paris; UNESCO, 1977 p. 34.

19

Whither Our Documentary Heritage

DOCUMENTARY SOURCES

Since the time immemorial human beings were communicating with each other through gestures, symbols, sounds, words and written and printed books and of late through electronic media. The written, printed and electronic media enabled human thought to be communicated through physical entities called documents and made it fit for transport across space and time. In this physical form human thought is transmitted from one point to any other point on earth, and is preserved for pretty long time. Documentary sources enabled human civilisation to communicate with one another and thus enrich themselves with the help of this communication processes. Through, centuries human thought is embodied and represented in various forms of documentary sources such as books, journals, manuscripts of various types, news papers and non-book materials to mention a few. During two thousand years of human civilisation, and even before, it was evident that the intellectual products of human thought and endeavor were being procured processed and preserved in various types of libraries through out the world. The world's great libraries viz: National, Public, Academic, Special, and Institutional are examples of repositories of human civilization and culture.

INDIA'S RICH DOCUMENTARY HERITAGE

India, the cradle of highly developed civilisation and culture is dotted with variety of libraries in various parts of the country. The growth and development of these libraries accelerated during the last two centuries. During the Moghul and the British rule several libraries especially Public, Academic and Institutional have been established at important centers of learning in the country, These libraries possess rich, varied and very valuable documentary collections reflecting political, social, economic and cultural aspects of the country and its people. In essence the documentary sources available in some of the very prominent and oldest libraries represent and reflect India's cultural heritage in particular and worlds heritage in general

The emerging knowledge society not only depends upon food, shelter and clothing but also very much on information/ knowledge to satisfy its intellectual needs. There are varieties of information/knowledge sources, which the present day society needs for its growth and development Every society must be in a position to know its past cultural heritage and contributions in various fields of human endeavor. The past will act as a stimulus for the present as well as the future developments in society. India's rich cultural heritage is embodied in various types of documentary sources possessed by very old and famous libraries existing in various parts of the country. This rich and glorious documentary heritage needs to he properly surveyed, preserved, processed and disseminated to the present as well as "future generations.

SCOPE OF DOCUMENTARY HERITAGE

The phrase documentary heritage denotes a simple document, a collection, a holding or archival fonds. A document has two facets or/and components. The information contains and the medium which supports it. They embody different forms of information and may be supported on different storage media.

These includes :

1. Textual material such as books, Mss, newspapers, papyrus, plastic, parchment, palm leaves, bark, textile, silk, store or other media,
2. Non-textual materials such as drawings, print, maps, music etc. The physical support is similar to those of textual material.
3. Traditional moving and still photographic images. The physical supports are usually paper or plastic but may be metal or glass and
4. Electronic data of all types including audio, video and text. The physical support is usually in sound form of plastic, metals or glass.

PROMINENT LIBRARIES IN SOUTH INDIA

Some of the oldest and prominent libraries in South India (this is true with other parts of the country) possess rich, varied, rare and invaluable documentary sources, which require immediate attention and action for preservation and conservation. 'These libraries include State Central Libraries, Regional Libraries. Oriental Manuscript Libraries and libraries attached to Educational Institutions. Research Centers, Religious/Cultural organisations, Learned Societies and libraries managed by private organisations. To be more specific mention may be made of few very old and prominent libraries in *Andhra Pradesh:* State Central Library, Hyderabad, Sarawata Niketnam Vetapalam, Vardhamana Samajam Library, Nellore and Gautami Grandhalayam, Rajamundry, *Tamilnadu :* Connemera Public Library, Chennai, Adyar Library and Research Center, Chennai, IMS Sarwasthi Mahal Library, Thanjavoor, Dr. U.V. Swaminath Iyer Library, Banglore, Oriental Research Institute Library Mysore, Kannada Research Institute Library, Dharwad, Karwar General Library, Karwar, *Kerala :* Trivandrum Public Library, Ernakulam Public Library, Kochi, Oriental Research Institute and Manuscript Library,

University of Kerala, Trivandrum and kerala Sahitya Acadey Library, Thrissur. The list is not exhaustive but illustrative. The rich documentary collections possessed by these libraries not only needs to be safeguarded but also the access to this heritage needs to be democratized so as to bring awareness of its significance to the people in general and the intellectuals in particular.

This documentary heritage includes paper and palm leaf manuscripts, very old printed books, back volumes of periodicals, reports, news papers, paintings, illustrations and illustrated manuscripts. The paper and palm leaf manuscripts are in Sanskrit, Tamil, Telugu, Kannada, Malayalam, Arabic, Persian, Urdu and Marathi. A variety of subjects in the fields of Sciences, Arts, Humanities and Technologies are covered by these manuscripts, printed books and other types of documents. The rich and varied collections deal with branches of Philosophy. Religion. Culture, Fine Arts. Architecture, Medicine, Agriculture, literature, Linguistics, Music, Astrology, Astronomy and Technology.

The valuable collections of these libraries mirror the culture and civilization of India and the richness of Indian languages and also the social and political conditions of the people. These libraries regarded as social and cultural institutions of the nation reflect the documentary heritage of India in general and South Indian states in particular. There is an urgent need to conserve and preserve the documentary heritage. Laxity on the part of Central and State Governments may cause immense harm to this heritage. The protection and safeguards extended to out ancient sites, monuments and buildings through legislative and administrative measures must equally be extended to this documentary heritage.

UNESCO'S INITIATIVE

In such a scenario it is not out of place to mention the efforts of UNESCO in this regard. UNESCO in the year 1992 launched 'Memory of the World Programme' to protect and promote world documentary heritage. The objectives of this program are four fold: 1 to facilitate preservation by appropriate techniques, 2. to assist access to documentary heritage. 3. to increase awareness worldwide and 4. to promote the program and its products to the widest possible public[2]. Under this programme UNESCO under the contract with International Federation of Library Associations and Institutions (IFLA) has brought out three valuable documents viz. : 1. *Memory of the World: General guidelines to safeguard documentary heritage, 1995*[3] 2. Memory of the World: *A survey of current Library Preservation activities,* 1996[4] and 3. *Memory of the World: Lost Memory - Libraries and Archives destroyed in 20th Century,* 1996[5]. These three documents provide very valuable and authenticate information on World Documentary Heritage, its present status, guidelines for preservation and conservation.

WHAT NEEDS TO BE DONE

The authorities at the state and national levels must give due thought and attention to the state of affairs of documentary heritage available in some of She oldest and prominent libraries and initiate immediate action to safe guard such documentary heritage, which is in deteriorating condition. The managements of some of these libraries were not able to initiate proper action for preserving and conserving the documentary sources for want of government support. If the situation continues for long the present and future generations may loose forever our rich and varied documentary heritage. The Department of Culture, Ministry of Human Resource Development, Govt of India must float a national fund, as was clone in the case of World Heritage Sites, to assist the managements of these libraries to preserve and conserve the documentary heritage, The state governments also must lend a helping hand in this regard, Non-governmental organizations also can come forward to assist in this endeavour. UNSECO under its 'Memory of the World' program, may assist some of the oldest and prominent libraries to protect and preserve our documentary heritage for posterity.

REFERENCES

1. Memory of the world: General Guidelines to Safeguard Documentary Heritage. Paris, UNESCO 1995. p6
2. Ibid, p1
3. Ibid. 77pp
4. Memory of the World: A Surveys of Current Library Preservation Activities. Paris, UNESCO, 1996. 59pp
5. Lost Memory-Libraries and Archives Destroyed in the 20th century. Paris. UNESCO. 1996, 70pp

20

An Analysis of Festschrift Volumes in Library and Information Science

DEFINITIONS AND MEANING

The term *'festschrift'* borrowed from German means Celebration Publication. The *Oxford English Dictionary* (OED) defines *'festschrift'* as *"A collection of writings forming a volume presented to a scholar or savant on the occasion of his attaining a certain age or a period in his career"*. Definitions from the 'Web states that "a complimentary or memorial publication in the form of a collection of essays, addresses or biographical, bibliographical, scientific or other contributions, often embodying the results of research, issued in honor of a person, an institution or a society, and usually on the occasion of an anniversary celebration". Another definition states that "a memorial or complimentary volume issued in honor of a scholar. The theme is usually the subject area in which the individual distinguished himself or herself, and the essays are often written by former students, colleagues or admirers. A festschrift may also honor an institution or society usually on a significant anniversary". Significantly there is no entry under 'festschrift' in any one of the leading English language encyclopedias.

From these definitions one can infer that the person in whose honor a festschrift is brought out should be a 'Scholar' or 'Savant' and who has put his stamp on some branch of enquiry during a certain period of time. The theme of the festschrift is "usually the subject area in which the individual distinguished himself or herself". Festschrifts are generally brought out by former students, colleagues, followers or admirers on occasions such as attaining the age of superannuation or any other significant occasions.

FESTSCHRIFTS IN LIBRARY AND INFORMATION SCIENCE

The subject Library and Information Science has history of a century and half. It has grown from 'Art' to 'Science' due to the contributions of eminent personalities from all parts of the world. It has greatly expanded to cover the emerging fields such as Information and Communication Technologies. As for the contributions from India are concerned eminent librarians and teachers of LIS have contributed their intellectual might to enrich the literature on LIS. From among such eminent personalities who have put their 'stamp', Dr. S. R. Ranganathan stands tallest. His seminal contributions to various facets of LIS is unique and far reaching and has put his 'stamp' on every branch of LIS and contributed to the emergence of 'Indian School of Thought'. In addition to Dr. Ranganathan, there are other 'stalwarts' who have contributed in their own way for the advancement of LIS. These stalwarts in LIS had their own students, colleagues, admirers and followers. In honor of these stalwarts, festschrift volumes have been brought out during the last six decades.

NUMBER OF FESTSCHRIFT VOLUMES PUBLISHED

It is rather difficult to arrive at the correct number of festschrift volumes published in LIS so far in honour of Indian LIS personnel. Information gathered by the author of this article with the help of professional colleagues, the number comes close to fifty publications. This figure may not be correct. Some of the festschrift volumes published could not be located and identified. Most of the publications are in single volumes and few cases they are in two volumes. The earliest festschrift volume which has come to the notice is Dr. S. R. Ranganathan Festschrift volume brought out to commemorate his 71st Birthday. This is in two volumes - Vol-1: *Library Science Today: Ranqanathan Festschrift* edited by P. N. Kaula, 1965. Vol.2: *An Essay in Personal Bibliography: Ranganathan Festschrift: Bibliography of the writings on and by S. R. Ranganathan*, compiled by A. K. Dasgupta, 1967. Both the volumes were published by Asia Publishing House, Bombay. Eminent personalities both from India and abroad have contributed articles to Volume-1. Especially parts T to W, which deals with Evaluation (Works), Evaluation (Works and Life), Evaluation (Life) and Reminiscences throw light on Ranganathan's life and works. This Volume contains 121 articles covering various facets of Library Science including Life and Works of Ranganathan. The Volume-2 is a bibliography of works on and by Ranganathan very meticulously compiled by one of the senior most and eminent library professional A. K. Dasgupta whose contributions to our profession is well known. This is a model bibliography for any one to compile a Personal Bibliography. The two volumes stand as unique contributions to LIS and can be termed as *'magnumopus'* of festschrift volumes. It appears that festschrift volumes have been brought out in honour of S. N. Srivastav, Upadhyaya, S. R. Ganpule and C. P. Shukla. The bibliographical details were not ascertainable.

COVERAGE OF FESTSCHRIFT VOLUMES

As stated earlier "festschrifts are for men who have put in their stamp on *some branch of enquiry* during certain period of time". This means that the 'festschrift' volume to be brought out in some body's honour should confine to or deal with 'some branch(es) of enquiry' on which a person has put his / her stamp. But most of the festschrift volumes so far published cover or deal with various facets of LIS relegating the "Persons expertise / authority", if any, into the background. Majority of the volumes so far published are general in nature i.e. covering various branches of LIS. The reason for this trend perhaps may be that if the publications restricted to certain branch/es *or* area/s of the persons domain, it may be difficult to get the expected articles from the contributors. On the other hand, identifications of contributors who can contribute 'original / standard' articles on the selected branches / areas may be difficult. The other side of coin is that the person on whom a festschrift volume is being brought may not be an expert/authority in certain branch/es of LIS, but he/she is a generalise.

There are few publications which are confined to certain branch/es / area/s of US. Mostly these festschrift volumes deal with the emerging areas of LIS especially Information and Communication Technologies and Library Systems. In few cases the person/s may be an authority in the branch / area on which the volume has been brought out. But in certain cases it is the other way round. The subject area/s covered in the volume has no relevance as to the 'authority' or the 'expertise' of the person concerned.

It can be inferred from the festschrift volumes so far published that bringing out a volume covering various facets of LIS is more feasible, easier and safer than confining to certain area/s or branch/es of LIS. More contributors can come forward to contribute an article of their expertise or choice. Such volumes can be of use to LIS professionals at large.

GENERAL FESTSCHRIFT VOLUMES

As stated already out of forty eight festschrift volumes identified by this author of the article, majority of them say thirty one volumes come under this category. These volumes cover important branches of LIS including emerging areas such as: Computer Application, Information and Communication Technologies, Knowledge Societies, Library Networks and Digital Libraries and so on. The titles of these publications reflect this aspect or trend. For example: Library Science Today (Ranganathan

Festschrift); *Dimensions of Library and Information Science* (Kaula Festschrift); *Perspectives in Library and Information Science* (Viswanathan Festschrift); *Library and Information Sciences: Emerging Challenges* (Gidwani Festschrift); *In the Library and Information Science Horizon* (Kamath Festschrift); *Current Research in Library and Information Science* (Kumbhar Festschrift). The list of these *thirty one* festschrifts is given in Annexure-1.

SPECIFIC SUBJECT FESTSCHRIFT VOLUMES

It may be mentioned that few specific subject festschrift volumes haye been brought out covering areas such as: Academic, University and Public Libraries, Bibliographical Control, Multimedia, Electronic Libraries, Knowledge Organization, Information Technology and Computerization. Since the scope is restricted on specific area it is rather difficult to identify the contributors who can really contribute articles on the specific subject of the volume. The author of this article could identify eleven publications dealing with the specific subject areas listed above. In most of these volumes the total number of articles does not exceed thirty with exception to Prof. K. Sarada Festschrift which contains forty one articles in two volumes. The list of these eleven volumes is presented in Annexure-2.

COMMEMORATION VOLUMES

Generally a festschrift volume is brought out to present to a 'Scholar' or 'Savant' on the occasion of his attaining a certain age or a period of his career. In the case of commemoration / memorial volume it is brought out to preserve the memory of the person who is no more with us. In various branches of knowledge to commemorate or preserve the memory of an eminent person commemoration or memorial volume is brought out. US is no exception in this regard. Few commemoration volumes have been published by the well-wishers / friends / followers of the departed person. The author of this article could lay his hand on six of such publications. These are: *Developing Horizons in LIS* ;

Ranganathans Tenth Death Anniversary Commemoration Volumes; Information and Society : Essays in Memory of Prof. P. Gangadhara Rao; Phani Busan Roy Commemorative Volumes; Current Trends in Library fit information Services : Prof. K. S. Deshpandav Commemoration Volume; Library and Information Services in India : Dr. S. M. Ganguly Commemorative Volume and Policies, Culture and Society : Collection of Essays in Memory of S. M. Ganguly. It is heartening to note that two commemorative volumes have brought out on S. M. Ganguly by his admirers and followers. This shows the high esteem and love he holds amongst his followers. The list of the Commemorative Volumes in presented in **Annexure-3**.

MULTIVOLUME FESTSCHRIFTS

It has been found that majority of Festschrifts are single volume publications. But there are some multivolume publications we come across in LIS. The festschrifts brought out in honour of Personalities such as S. R. Ranganathan, O. R. Kalia, C. G. Vishwanathan, P.S.G. Kumar, K. Navlani, C. P. Vashishth, Mohd. Sabir Hussain, P. B. Mangla and K. Sarada *are* two volume publications.

EDITORS OF FESTSCHRIFT / COMMEMORATION VOLUMES

It is interesting to note that except few, the rest of the festschrift volumes have been edited by joint editors and in some cases by more than two editors. In one case there are five editors for a festschrift volume. If we take into consideration only the names of the first editor, it is found that Sarvasri C. P. Vashishth, K. Navlani, L. S. Ramaiah and A. A. N. Raju have edited two festschrift volumes each. In fact B. Ramesh Babu has edited three festschrift volumes. Names of some persons appear as joint editor's in more than one festschrift volume.

The analysis of the forty eight festschrifts has revealed that in honour of some persons more than one or two festschrifts have been brought out. The persons on whom such honour has been bestowed are: S. R. Ranganathan, P. N. Kaula, S. M. Ganguly, L. S.

Ramaiah and V. Venkatappaiah. In case of S. R. Ranganathan one is festschrift and the other is commemorative volume. In case of S. M. Ganguly both are commemorative volumes. As regards L. S. Ramaiah, both are festschrift volumes, in honour of Phani Bhusan Roy, the Bengal Library Association has brought out Commemorative Volume. This is the only instance where an Association has involved in bringing out a Festschrift Volume. The list of names of first editors along with names of the persons honoured by a festschrift is given in Annexure-4.

PUBLISHERS OF FESTSCHRIFT VOLUMES

Asia Publishing House has the honour of publishing Ranganathan Festschrift in the year 1965. Later on this leading Publishing House has disappeared from the publishing scene. In the last five decades many leading publishing houses have ventured to publish books in LIS.

As for publication of Festschrift Volumes are concerned Ess Ess Publications occupies the prime position by publishing eleven festschrift volumes (Nos. 1, 7, 10, 11, 12, 21, 27, 35, 36, 40 and 45)) in LIS. This is followed by Vikas (Nos. *2*, 25, 39), Concept (Nos. 5, 14, 20), Allied (Nos. 9, 33, 38, 43), T. R. Publications (Nos. 24, 32, 37) which have published three festschrifts each. This shows that the leading publishers of the Country have evinced interest in bringing out publications in LIS including Festschrift Volumes. The other Publishing Houses such as: RBSA Publishers (Nos. 3, 18), B. R. Publishing Co. (Nos. 6, 13), have brought two Festschrifts each. Other publishing houses such as: Print House (No.26), Y. K. Publishers (No.31), Madalion (No.42), Viva Books (No.30), Raj Publishing (No.28), Indian Bibliographic Centre (No.43), Authors Press (No.19), Print Well (No.44), Rawat (No. 17), Vaibhav (No. 16), New Age (No.48), Bengal Library Association (No.47) and iASLIC (No.46), Manak (4), Research Co. (8), Indus (15), Asia (22), Gyan (29), Cosmo (34) and UBS Publishers (44) have published one festschrift each. It is a fact that most of the leading Indian Publishing Houses are stationed in the National Capital New Delhi and their branch offices in the metropolitan cities of North and South India. From the South, mentioned may be made of T. R. Publications, Chennai, which has ventured to publish books in US including three festschrift volumes. The list of names of persons in whose honour the festschrifts have been brought out along with the names of first editors is presented in Annexute-5.

CONCLUSION

From the preceding paragraphs it can be concluded that a good number of festschrift volumes have been published in honour of LIS Professionals who have through their writings and services 'enriched' the field of LIS and put their 'stamp' on some branch of LIS during certain period of time. In certain cases it is not necessarily on the basis of the contributions / services of the person concerned but the initiative and interest of his / her followers / well-wishers / students festschrift volume has been brought out. This trend is very much visible and continuing. How long this trend will continue is difficult to predict. There are few instances where eminent personalities in LIS who have really put their stamp on some branch of LIS and rendered yeomen services have been completely forgotten. Is this due to lack of initiative and support from his / her followers and students or lack of 'Camp Followers'. In certain cases the honour has been bestowed not at the end of official Professional career but at the fag end of their lives. This may be due to lethargy of the profession in not recognizing the valuable contributions and services of such persons who definitely deserve a festschrift or commemoration volume. But one thing is certain that in the years to come the LIS profession may witness the proliferation of so called festschrift volumes. Is this trend augurs well for the profession? Only time can answer this question.

ANNEXURE-1

LIST OF GENERAL FESTSCHRIFT VOLUMES

(Arranged alphabetically by title)

1. Books to Bytes: Library and Information Technology in the New Millennium: Essays in honour of *Prof. I S. Ramaiah.* Ed. By N. V. Jagga Rao and M. Ramchander. New Delhi, Ess Ess Publications, 2000. Rs.900.00. XXVI, 433 p.
2. Comparative Librarianship : Essay in honour of *Prof. D. N. Marshall.* Ed by N. N. Gidwani, Delhi, Vikas Publishing House, 1973. 243p.
3. Current Research in Library and Information Science : Festschrift to *Prof. M. R. Kumbhar.* Ed by S. Seetharama and C. R. Karisiddappa. Jaipur, RBSA Publishers, 1993. 196p.
4. Current Studies in Library and Information Science : Felicitation Volume of *Dr. S. R. Gunjal.* Ed by C. R. Karisiddappa et al. Delhi, Manak Publications, 1993. IX, 352p.
5. Dimensions of Library and Information Science. *Kaula Festschrift.* Ed by Velaga Venkatappaiah et al. New Delhi, Concept, 1990. Rs.600.00.
6. Information, Communication, Library and Community Development: Festschrift in honour of *Prof. C. P. Vashishth.* Ed by B. Ramesh Babu and S. Gopalakrishnan. Delhi; B. R. Publishing Corporation. 2004. 2 Vols. XXV, 777p.
7. Information Management, Sources and other Studies: Essays in honour of *Prof. K. Navlani.* Vol. II. Ed by. Ashu Shokeen, et al. New Delhi, Ess Ess Publications, 2001. Rs. 1500.00, XVI, 238p.
8. Information Management: Trends and Issues: Festschrift in honour of *Prof. S. Seetarama.* Ed by B. Ramesh Babu, A. A. Vaishnav and S. Gopalakrishnan. New Delhi, Research Co Book Centre, 2004. 500p.

9. In the Library and Information Science Horizon: A Collection of Essays in honour of *Dr. V. A. Kamath.* Presented by Bombay Science Library Association (BOSLA). Ed by B. Guha. New Delhi, Allied Publishers, 1986. XIV, 433p.

10. Knowledge Management: Today and Tomorrow. Festschrift in honour of *Dr. Velaqa Venkatappayya* on the occasion of his 71st Birthday. Ed by B. Ramesh Babu and S. Gopalakrishan. New Delhi, Ess Ess Publications, 2003. Rs.900.00, 412p.

11. Knowledge Societies and Libraries: Papers in honour of *Prof. A. A. N. Raju.* Ed by N. Laxman Rao, et al. New Delhi, Ess Ess Publications, 2004. Rs. 1075.00. XXVI, 517p.

12. Librarianship and Library Science Education. Essays in Honour of *Dr. J. S. Shqrma.* Ed by Seva Singh. New Delhi, Ess Ess Publications, 1988.

13. Library and Information Profession in India : *Dr. P. S. G. Kumar* Festschrift. V2: Assessment of the Man and His Works. By C. P. Vashishth et al. Delhi, B, R. Publishing Corporation, 2004, 258p.

14. Library and Information Science: Parameters and Perspectives. Festschrift in honour *of Prof.P. B. Manila. 2* Vols. Ed by R. G. Prasher. New Delhi, Concept Publishing House, 1997.

15. Library and Information Science: Trends and Challenges: Essay in honour of *Prof.* S. *S. Agrawal* Ed by A. Tejomurthy and S. Kumar, New Delhi, Indus Publishing Co, 1993.

16. Library and Information Science— Some Perspectives : Festschrift in honour of Sri S. *Panduranga Reddy.* Ed by M. Sankara Reddy et al. (Bilingual). Hyderabad, Vaibhav Agencies, 1998. Rs.200.00. XXII, 256p.

17. Library and Information Sciences. Festschrift for *Dr. Ms. Anand and K. Anand.* Ed by K. Navlani and Sudha Trikha. New Delhi, Rawat Publications, 1999.

18. Library and Information Services: Emerging Challenges : Essays in honour of *N. N. Gidwani.* Ed by K. Navalani and M. P. Satija. Jaipur, RBSA Publishers, 1996. 268p.

19. Library and Information Studies in Cyber Age : Essays in honour of *Prof. J. L Sardana.* Ed by S. M. Dhawan. Delhi, Authors Press, 2004. Rs.995.00. XXIII, 606p.

20. Libraries and Information Studies in Retrospect and Prospect: Essay in honour of *Prof. D. R. Kalia.* Ed by J. L. Sardana, New Delhi, Concept Publishing Co., 2002. Rs. 1900/-. XXXV, 304p. 2 Vols.

21. Library Science and its Facets. *Prof. Mohd Sabir Hussain* Festschrift 2 vols. Ed by H. R. Chopra et al. New Delhi, Ess Ess Publications, 1998. Rs.900.00.

22. Library Science today. *Ranqanathan* Festschrift Vol.1. Papers contributed on the 71st Birthday of Dr. S. R. Ranganathan (12th August, 1962). Ed. By P. N. Kaula. Bombay, Asia Publishing House, 1965. Rs.65.00. 832p.

23. The Lotus Petals: A Profile of *Prof. P. N. Kaula.* Ed by S. R. Gupta. New Delhi, International Kaula Felicitation Committee, 1994.

24. New Horizons in Library and Information Science. *Dr. Velaqa Venkatappa* Festschrift. Ed by C. P. Vashishth, et al. Chennai, T. R. Publications, 1994. Rs.425.00. XXVIII, 602p.

25. New Vistas in Library and Information Science : Papers in honour of *Prof. G. V. S. L Narasimha Raju.* Ed by: A. A. N. Raju, et al. New Delhi, Vikas Publishing House, 1995. Rs.595.00. XXXVI, 600p.

26. Perspectives in Library and Information Science : *Viswanathan* Festschrift. 2. Vols. Ed by: S. N. Agarwal, et al. Lucknow, Print House (India), 1982. Rs.250.00. Vol.I. XVIII, 408 p. Vol.2. XXII, 215p.

27. Professional Librarianship : *C. A. Augstine* Festschrift. Ed. By G. Devarajan, et al. New Delhi, Ess Ess Publications, 1991. Rs.150.00. XIII, 119 p.

28. Readings in Library and Information Science : *Dr. S. P. Sood* Festschrift. Ed by S. D. Vyas, et al. Jaipur, Raj Publishing House, 2000. Rs.550.00. V, 299p.

29. Trends in Library and Information Science: Essays in Honour of *Prof. G. D. Bharqav.* Ed by Surendra Singh and Sonal Singh. New Delhi, Gyan Publishing House, 2000.

30. Vision of Future Library and Information Systems. *Dr.* S. S. *Murthy* Festschrift. Ed by T. Ashok Babu, et al. New Delhi, Viva Books, 2000. XIX, 265p.

31. Vistas in Library, Information Systems and Networks : A festschrift to *Prof.* S. *M. Tripathi.* Ed by M. V. Venugopal, et al. Agra, Y. K. Publishers, 1999. Rs.800.00. XXVIII, 381 p.

ANNEXURE-2

LIST OF SPECIFIC SUBJECT FESTSCHRIFT VOLUMES

(Arranged alphabetically by title)

1. Academic Libraries: Role in the National Development: Festschrift Volume in honour of *Prof. N. B. Inamdar.* Ed by Dorothy Isaac, et al. Chennai, T. R. Publications, 1993. Rs.270.00. XX, 304p.
2. Electronic Libraries. *Dr. P. Sadasivamurthy* Festschrift. Ed by Sangayya S. Sirumath et at. New Delhi, Allied Publishers, 2002. Rs.490/-. XIII, 216p.
3. Information Technology: Issues and G Trends. Festschrift in honour of *Prof. N.* Guruswamy *Naidu.* Ed by B. Satyanarayana, B. Ramesh Babu, et al. New Delhi, Cosmo Publications, 1998. 413p. 2 Vols. Rs. 2000.00.
4. Knowledge Organisation, Information Systems and other Essays. *Prof. A. Neelameqhan* Festschrift. Ed by K. S. Raghavan and K. N. Prasad. New Delhi, Ess Ess Publications, 2005. Rs. 1125.00.
5. Library Computerization in India. *Isaac* Festschrift. Ed by G. Devarajan and A. V L. rehalamma. New Delhi, Ess Ess Publications, 1990.
6. Multimedia - Its applications in Library and Information Science : Festschrift in honour of *Prof. L. S. Ramaiah.* Ed by B. Satyanarayana, et al. Chennai, T. R. Publications, 1998. Rs.295.00. XVI, 267p.
7. National Bibliographical Control: Problems and Perspectives : Essays for *A. K Dasqupta.* Ed by A. A. N. Raju and L. S. Ramaiah. New Delhi, Allied Publishers, 2003. Rs. 380.00. XX, 430p.
8. Public Libraries in Developing Countries: Status and Trends: *Or, B. P. Barua* Festschrift Volume. Ed by P. K. Mahapatra and V . Thomas. New Delhi, Vikas Publishing House, 1996. XIX, 252p.

9. Public Library System: Services and Networking. *K Sarada* Festschrift. Ed by L. S. Ramaiah et al. New Delhi, Ess Ess Publications, 1997, 2 Vols. (Vol.1 289p, Vol.2 233p).

10. University and College Librarianship in India in the 21st Century. *Prof. S. G. Mahajan* Festschrift. Ed by Neela J. Deshpandey and S. K. Patil, Pune, S. G. Mahajan Felicitation Committee,2004. Rs.600.00, 333p.

11. University Libraries in India 1980s and Beyond : Essay in honour of *Prof. T. P. Saxena.* Ed by R. G. Prasher. New Delhi, Medallion Press, 1991, 285p.

12. Developing Cyber Libraries : Festschrifts in honor of Prof. M. Sankara Reddy. Ed. by T. Ashok Babu and L.S. Ramaiah, New Delhi, Allied, 2006.

13. Digital Information Resources and Networks on India : Essays in honour of Prof., J.S. Ramdev. Ed. by R.S. Chalan et.al., New Delhi, UBS Publishers, 2006.

ANNEXURE-3

LIST OF COMMEMORATION VOLUMES

(Arranged Alphabetically by Title)

1. Current Problems and Trends in Library and Information Services : *Prof. K.S. Deshpandey* Commemoration Volume. Ed by H. A. Khan and S. R. Ijari. Varanasi, Indian Bibliographic Centre, 1990. 366p.
2. Developing Horizons in Library and Information science: *Ranganathan's Tenth Death Anniversary Commemoration Volumes.* 2 Vols. Ed by C. D. Sharma and Kailash Vyas. Jaipur, Printwell Publishers, 1983. Vol.1 XII, Rs.98.00, 252p. Vol.2. XVI, Rs.122.00, 299p.
3. Information and Society : Essays in Memory of *Prof. P. Gangadhara Rao.* Ed by L. S. Ramaiah, et al. New Delhi, Ess Ess Publications, 1997. Rs.650.00, XXVI, 409p.
4. Library and Information Services in India : *Dr. S. M. Ganguly* Commemorative Volume. Ed by Prabir Roy Choudhury and Nirmalendu Mukhopadhyaya. Calcutta, IASLIC, 2000. Rs.250.00. 336p.
5. *Phani Bhusan Roy* Commemoratie Volume. Ed by Bengal Library Association. Kolkata, BLA, 1998. 284p.
6. Policies, Culture and Society : Collection of Essays in memory of *S. M. Ganguly.* Ed by Arindra Mohan Ghos et al. Kolkata, New Age Publications, 2005, X, 340p.

ANNEXURE-4

NAME OF THE FIRST EDITOR
(Arranged alphabetically)

	Name of the First Editor	Name of the person honored with Festschrift
1.	S. N. Agarwal	*C. G. Vishwanathan*
2.	T. Ashok Babu	*S. S. Murthy*
3.	Bengal Library Association	*P. B. Roy*
4.	H. R. Chopra	*Mohd. Sabir Hussain*
5.	N. J. Deshpandey	*S. G. Mahajan*
6.	G. Devarajan	*K. A. Isaac*
7.	G. Devarajan	*C. A. Augustine*
8.	S. M. Dhavan	*J. L Sardana*
9.	N. N. Gidwani	*J. N. Marshall*
10.	S. R. Gupta ..	*P. N. Kaula*
11.	A. M. Ghosh..	*S. M. Ganguly*
12.	B. Guha	*V. A. Kamath*
13.	Dorothy Isaac	*N. B. Inamdar*
14.	N. V. Jagga Rao	*L S. Ramaiah*
15.	C. R. Karisiddappa	*S. R. Gunjal*
16.	P. N. Kaula ..	*S. R. Ranganathan*
17.	H. A. Khan ..	*K. S. Deshpandey*
18.	N. Laxman Rao	*A. A. N. Raju*
19.	P. K. Mahapatra	*B. P. Barua*
20.	K. Navlani	*A. K. Anandan & K. Anand*
21.	K. Navlani	*N. N. Gidwani*
22.	R. G. Prasher	*P. B. Mangla*
23.	R. G. Prasher	*T. P. Saxena*
24.	K. S. Raghavan	*A. Neelameghan*

	Name of the First Editor	Name of the person honored with Festschrift
25.	A. A. N. Raju	*G. V. S. L Narasimha Raju*
26.	A. A. N. Raju	*A. K. Dasgupta*
27.	L. S. Rarnaiah	*K Sarada*
28.	L. S. Ramaiah	*P. Gangadhara Rao*
29.	B. Ramesh Babu	*C. P. Vashishth*
30.	B. Ramesh Babu	*S. Seeta Rama*
31.	B. Ramesh Babu	*V. Venkatappaiah*
32.	M. Sankar Reddy	*S. P. Ranga Reddy*
33.	J. L. Sardana	*D. R. Kalia*
34.	B.Satyanarayana	*L. S. Ramaiah*
35.	B. Satyanarayana	*N. Guruswamy Naidu*
36.	S. Seetarama	*M. R. Kumbhar*
37.	A. Seva Singh	*J. S. Sharma*
38.	Ashu Shokeen	*K. Navlani*
39.	S. S. Sirumath	*Sadasiva Murthy*
40.	A. Surendra Singh	*G. D. Bhargav*
41.	A. Tejomurthy	*S. S. Agrawal*
42.	C. P. Vashishth	*P. S. G. Kumar*
43.	C. P. Vashishth	*V. Venkatappaiah*
44.	V. Venkatappaiah	*P. N. Kaula*
45.	M. V. Venujgopal	*S. M. Tripathi*
46.	S. D. Vyas ..	*S. P. Sood*
47.	Prabir Roy Choudhury	*S. M. Ganguly*
48.	C. D. Sharrna	*S. R. Ranganathan*
49.	T. Ashok Babu	*M. Sankar Reddy*
50.	R.S. Chilana	*Joginder Singh Ram Dev*

ANNEXURE-5

	Name of the Person honored With Festschrift (arranged alphabetically)	Name of the First Editor:
1.	S. S. Agarwal	*A. Tejomurthy*
2.	A. K. Anand and K. Anand	*K. Navlani*
3.	C. A. Augustine	*G. Devarajan*
4.	B. P. Barua	*P. K. Mahapatra*
5.	G. D. Bhargav	*Surendra Singh*
6.	A. K. Dasgupta	*A. A. N. Raju*
7.	K. S. Desh Pandey	*H. A. Khan*
8.	P. Gangadhara Rao	*L S. Ramaiah*
9.	S. M. Ganguly	*A M. Ghosh*
10.	S. M. Ganguly	*Prabin Roy Choudhury*
11.	N. N. Gidwani	*K. Navlani*
12.	S. R. Gunjal	*C. R. Karisiddappa*
13.	N. Guruswamy Naidu	*B. Saya*noroyana
14.	Mohd. Sabir Hussain	*H. R. Chopra*
15.	N. B. Inamdar	*Dorothy Isaac*
16.	K. A. Isaac	*G. Devarajan*
17.	D. R. Kalia	*J. L. Sardana*
18.	V. A. Kamath	*B. Guha*
19.	P. N. Kaula	*S.R.Gupta*
20.	P. N. Kaula	*V. Venkatappaiah*
21.	P. S. G. Kumar	*C. P. Vashishth*

Name of the Person honored With Festschrift (arranged alphabetically)	Name of the First Editor:
22. M. R. Kumbhar	*S. Seetarama*
23. S. G. Mahajan	*N. J. Oeshpandey*
24. P. B. Mangla	*R. G. Prashar*
25. J. N. Marshall	*N. N. Gidwani*
26. S. S. Murthy	*T. Ashok Babu*
27. G. V. S. L. Narasimha Raju	*A. A. N. Raju*
28. K. Navlani ..	*Ashu Shokeen*
29. A. Neelameghan	*K. S. Raghavan*
30. A. A. N. Raju	*N. Laxman Rao*
31. L. S. Ramaiah	*N. V. Jagga Rao*
32. L S. Ramaiah	*B. Satanarayana*
33. S. R. Ranganathan	*P. N. Kaula*
34. S. R. Ranganathan	*C. D. Sharma*
35. S. P. Ranga Reddy	*M. Sankar Reddy*
36. P. B. Roy	*Bengal Library Asso.*
37. Sadasiva Murthy	*S. S. Sirumath*
38. K. Sarada ..	*L S. Ramaiah*
39. J. L. Sardana	*S. M. Dhavan*
40. T. P, Saxena	*R. G. Prasher*
41. S. Seetarama	*S. Ramesh Babu*
42. J. S. Sharma	*Sewa Singh*
43. S. P. Sood ..	*S. D. Vyas*

	Name of the Person honored With Festschrift (arranged alphabetically)	Name of the First Editor:
44.	S. M. Tripathi	*M. V. Venugopal*
45.	C. P. Vashishth	*B. Ramesh Babu*
46.	V. Venkatappaiah	*B. Ramesh Babu*
47.	V. Venkatappaiah	*C. P. Vashishth*
48.	C. G. Vishwanathan	*S. N. Agarwal*
49.	M. Sankara Reddy	*T. Ashok Babu*
50.	Joginder Sing Ram Dev	*Rajwant Singh Chilana*

21
Need for Good Library Support Services to Distance Learners

WHO ARE DISTANCE LEARNERS (DLS)?

There is no one meaning for the term Distance Education. It is known by variety of names Viz:'Correspondence education',' Home study', 'Independent study', 'External study', 'Off-Campus study', 'Open learning', 'Open education' etc. In India those who are concerned with this type of education have been using 'External appearance' (Private appearance),'Correspondence education' and Distance education (DE).[1] Experts in the field have made subtle distinction between these three terms. However the term Distance Education has gained ground and established in the field. Those who pursue this type of education are called distance learners (DLs) and fall under the following categories[2]:

1. Students who had to discontinue their formal education due to various reasons,
2. Students in geographically remote areas
3. Students who had to discontinue their education for lack of aptitude and motivation but who may later get motivated,

4. Students who cannot be admitted or who do not wish to pursue a course at regular colleges and universities,
5. In-service persons and,
6. Individuals who think education is a life long activity and would like to pursue their own field of interest or new fields/ disciplines

CHARACTERISTICS OF DISTANCE LEARNERS

DLs to a larger extent are motivated and matured adults representing different socio-economic, cultural, educational and linguistic backgrounds. They differ widely in age, qualifications, aspirations, interests and tastes. They are fully or partially employed, retired, single, married, housewives and disabled. The learning process and activity of these persons is part time which takes place in leisure hours, in evenings or holidays. These may either study individually at home, in a library or in groups at Study Centers of DE Institutions attending counseling and contact programmes[3]. These characteristics may have some bearing on the collections and services of LICs of DE Institutions. Of late young graduates who were not able to get admission in conventional colleges and universities for higher studies are enrolling as distance learners so as to not to waste their precious academic year.

IMPORTANCE OF LIBRARY AND INFORMATION SERVICES

DE is a student-centered education and not a teacher centered education as we find in the conventional Schools, Colleges and Universities. In a teacher centered education the teacher is a friend, philosopher and guide. Mostly the learners depend upon the lectures delivered and/or 'notes' dictated by the teacher. Their dependence on Lib & Inf. Services is not very much felt with exception to few serious students and subject fields. On the contrary a distance learner is his own Boswell. His attending to counseling/Contact classes is for guidance and seeking clarifications from the course material supplied to him/her. It is not time bound. He can pursue at his own pace. Attending counseling classes is not compulsory. His/Her dependence upon the course material and the guidance he/she gets from the Counselors/Tutors must be supplemented and complimented by good Library and Information Services. There fore a distance learner is very much dependent on very effective Lib & Inf. Services to improve the quality of assignments, projects and a better performance in the examinations.

NEED FOR LIBRARY AND INFORMATION SERVICES

As stated earlier in addition to course materials the next most important supporting service to a DLs is Lib & Inf. Services. DLs requires access to library resources/services for reference on the premises and for study at home. DLs pursuing courses for higher degrees have to depend on additional reading materials suggested/recommended at the end of each Unit/Block in the course material. It would be more helpful if the LICs of DE Institutions equip with the following types of reading materials and facilities[4]:

1. Reference and Information Sources covering the courses offered by DE Institution/s,
2. Self instructional course materials and study packages developed by various DE Institutions in the country and abroad,
3. AV/Non-Print materials brought out by various Organisations and Institutions in the country and abroad.
4. AV Equipment, Photocopying facilities, Microfilimreader cum printer, computer etc
5. Independent and appropriately equipped room for DLs to meet and to listen/view audio and video programmes.
6. Non-print media to support the print media, and
7. Internet accesses facility.

NEED FOR GOOD LIBRARY SUPPORT AT STUDY CENTERS

A study center is a part of an over all system of support for

DLs. It is a place, which is open for attendance of DLs. DLs may come for counseling, contact programmes, seminars, private study or for meeting with a Counselors/Tutor. As this is the focal point in the entire system of DE, it should be strengthened with a good library stocked with useful and appropriate collections, supported by infrastructure facilities and managed by qualified library staff. But in reality most of the Study Centers are not well supported by a good library. These have been functioning as weak links in he chain and were not able to meet the varied information needs of DLs. The Central Library at the headquarters may not be able to meet the information requirements of DLs who are scattered through the length and breadth of the State/Country.

In majority of the study centers there is no independent library managed by professionally qualified librarian. The collection is kept in few shelves or cupboards and looked after by the office assistant of the study center. Mostly the collection is under lock and key. The use of the library collection by the DLs after counseling/contact classes is almost nil or very much restricted. As the counseling classes go four to five hours a day practically the DLs find no time or inclination to stay longer for consulting the library collections to supplement and compliment the course material and for preparation and submission of assignments and project work. Majority of these study centers are closed after office hours and therefore there is no opportunity to those DLs who wish to stay longer hours to use the collections after office hours.

USE OF PUBLIC AND COLLEGE LIBRARY FACILITIES

In majority of urban, semi urban and rural areas we find a network of public libraries functioning at district, taluka, and village levels. For example Andhra Pradesh has a good network of public libraries functioning throughout the state. Even in rural areas a number of junior colleges and degree colleges have been established with library facilities. DLs are not only from the towns and cities, but also from rural areas. The participation of DLs in the counseling/contact programs is not encouraging. They very much depend upon the course material. To submit quality assignments some of the DLs may go beyond the course material and wish to consult other textbooks, reference books and back volumes of periodicals. Since some of the DLs especially from the rural areas are away from the study centers the nearest library facility available to them is a public/college library functioning in the vicinity of their habitat. Therefore and understanding has to be reached between the public/college library authorities and DE Institutions/Study Centers for cooperation between them to extend library services to DLs. DE institutions on their part can open a Cell to stock the learning resources which include in addition to course material, AV material, text books and reference books which may be of use to DLs for improving the quality of assignments/projects and also for better performances in the written examination. This type of cooperative arrangement will go a long way to extend the much needed library support services to DLs. The success of this proposition very much depends upon the cooperation extended by the public and college library authorities[5].

LIBRARY SUPPORT TO DE STAFF

In addition to the limited full time staff most of DE Institutions depend very much upon part time staff for counseling/ contact programmes. As for preparation of course materials also mostly out side faculty members are involved. For bringing out quality course material and for effective counseling/contact programmes the Central Library and Study Centers libraries must be in a position to offer qualitative Lib & Inf. Services to the part time staff. It is not that the resources available in other LICs are not used but it should be the primary responsibility of the main library and study centers libraries to support the information requirements of part time staff as well as course writers/editors. The part time staff also be invited to work shops, seminars and conferences organized for the benefit of full time staff by the DE institutions.

DE has come a long way in the country and elsewhere. Given the nature and the characteristics of DLs effective Lib & Inf. Services are sine-quo-non-for turning out quality products. There is an urgent need for strengthening the library and its services at the Study Centers. In view of introducing professional and technical courses and research programmes like M. Phil & Ph.D., the value and importance of Lib & Inf. Services cannot be over emphasized. The DLs and those involved in distance teaching, writing and research must be assured of well stocked, equipped and managed LICs and services. The emerging Information Technology also would greatly contribute to this endeavor.

REFERENCES

1. Ram Reddy, G., Distance education: what, why and how ? (In Readings in Distance Education-1. New Delhi, IGNOU, 1987. p 33).
2. Ibid, p 37
3. Neela Jagannathan: Libraries in Distance Education. *Indian Journal of Open Learning*. V1, N2, July 1992. p 34.
4. Ibid. P 34.
5. Raju A.A.N: Need for strengthening library and information services to distance learners. Paper presented to the seminar on Library and Information services to distance learners organized by Academy of Library Science and Documentation on 4th June 2000 at Hyderabad.

22
Teaching of Reference Service For B.Lib.Sc.

INTRODUCTION

The Institution of postgraduate Diploma course in Library Science at Osmania University goes back to the year 1959. For three years the course was conducted on part-time basis up to the end of academic year 1964-65. In keeping abreast with trends in Education for Librarianship, Diploma course in Library Science was upgraded into Degree Course from the academic year 1965-66 and in the same year a separate Department for Library Science was established. Since then B Lib Sc course is being conducted at the Osmania University. Presently the Department is located in the first floor of the University Library Building.

The course of B Lib Sc consists of 8 papers of 100 marks each. In addition to the 8 papers carrying 800 marks, Class Assignments carry 100 marks. The subject 'Reference Service' forms part of the whole paper 'Book Selection and Reference Service ' which is paper V in the syllabus of the course.

LIST OF TOPICS IN REFERENCE SERVICE

The syllabus of B Lib Sc course of Osmania University lists the following topics in Reference.

1. Introduction—what is reference work —the different functions of 'reference'; what is a reference bock.
2. Different types of reference books—value, point for evaluation of each type and important examples in each type—dictionaries; encyclopaedias; almanacs and year-books; biographical dictionaries; geographical reference books (atlas, gazetters, etc); hand-books and manuals; periodical lists and indexes; summaries; abstracting journals; government publications; bibliographies (bibliographies of bibliographies, national and trade bibliographies, subject bibliographies).
3. Evaluation and selection of reference book-sources.
4. Ready reference service vs long-range reference service.
5. Display method reading lists.

TEACHING PROGRAMME

The teaching programme of B Lib Sc course is spread over one academic year as the semester system was not followed. As already pointed out elsewhere, the subject reference service being part of the paper ' Book Selection and Reference Service ' two hours (each hour 50 minutes) are alloted per week for teaching the subject in addition to the practical work to be done in the Reference Department of the Library.

TEACHING METHODS

Reference Service is ' heart' and ' soul' of Library Science. The library techniques that are taught separately through other papers in B Lib Sc course, should be brought into relation with Reference Service' in all possible ways in order to drive home to the students the utility of these techniques in rendering effective Reference Service. This in turn will sprout interest among the students for learning the techniques. In reference work finding out of information from the documents is only half the battle. The other half of the battle lies in work with reader *i. e.,* in eliciting tactfully his/her exact needs and requirements and keeping him/

her in good humour till he/she is rendered all the service possible from the available Reference Sources. To do this type of personal service, requires the understanding the nuances and patterns of human relations, psychological patterns, and also modes and moods of the readers. To train the students to understand the highways and byways of reference service and of human relations, S R Ranganathan has suggested the following seven techniques of teaching of reference service.

1. Clinical method in the floor of the library;
2. Discussion method in the class room;
3. Preparatory work with reference books;
4. Find-me-out method;
5. Practical or workshop method;
6. Lecture method ; and
7. Case study method.

In the succeeding paras (31-34), some of the teaching methods that are being followed in the Department of Library Science, Osmania University is briefly discussed.

DISCUSSION METHOD

At the beginning of academic year, the students are introduced to the subject Reference Service and its place and importance in the field of Library Science and also its contribution for the welfare of human society. After one or two introductory lectures on the subject the students are introduced to the Reference Department of the University Library. Here the method of arrangement of Reference books and various types of Reference work which are to be discussed in the class room are shown to the students. With this, the students would participate with eagerness and curiosity in the discussion of the what, the why and the how of Reference Service. In this discussion method it can be clearly explained to the students with ease what is a reference work and how it differs from other works. This is one of the best and proven methods in education. It makes the students active participants in the learning process. In this process of the teacher acts as a discussion leader. The teacher should put some questions pertaining to the topic or the Reference tool discussed, which would create a sort of ripple of views or solutions from the students. The teacher should listen the students patiently and carefully and guide them on the right track. This method would develop in both the teacher and the taught creative thinking and an analytical mind. It will have advantage of collective thinking. This method acts as a touchstone and helps the teacher to know the potentialities of each of the students.

PREPARATORY WORK

In this method, the teacher acquaints the students formerly, with various types of Reference materials listed in Para 1 Item 2. This work is to be preceded by discussion method. In this each category of Reference materials (viz, Dictionaries, Encyclopaedias, etc) are studied systematically with the help and guidance of the teacher. Sufficient time should be given to the students for their a systematic study and assimilation of various types of Reference books, and this can be done within the specified time so that the available time can be evenly spread throughout the academic year to cover all types of Reference materials. It is better to provide a work sheet which may be of help to the students for the systematic study of Reference works and for record. A specimen work sheet is appended (see appendix 1). These work sheets are to be verified by the teacher at regular intervals.

FIND-ME-OUT METHOD

This method is very useful to familiarise the students with the ins and outs of Reference works. After the completion of a particular category of Reference works, specimen questions are framed and given to the students for finding answers from the Reference sources. This method makes the students to ' talk ' and make friendship with the various Reference sources. While framing the specimen questions, the teacher should keep in his mind the following points:

1. The sources for answering the questions must be available in the library;
2. The questions should confine to those type of reference works covered in the class;
3. The questions so framed should yield answer from not more than 3 or 4 reference works;
4. The questions should be graded and may be confined initially to Ready Reference Service and gradually questions pertaining to Long Range Reference Service can be framed; and
5. While framing the question the teacher should keep in mind the general educational standard of the students.

To record the students approach for answering the Reference questions, they should be provided with work sheets. The students may be instructed to record the number of sources for answering the question in their order of preference, with full bibliographical details and time taken for answering each question. They can also write about their pleasant surprises, disappoints failures or accidental successes. In this process, the teacher should be present in the Reference Department, so as to guide the students in times of need. The answered work sheets of each student should be gone through in his presence by the teacher and discuss with him and enlighten him wherever possible (see Appendix 2—model find-me-out questions Appendix 3 : Model work sheet for answering Find-me-out Questions).

In addition to drill the students in Find-me-out method at regular intervals as per the coverage of the syllabus three ' Reference Quiz ' tests are conducted in the Department of Library Science, Osmania University. The duration of each Test is for one hour in which five questions are given. Each student gels a different set of questions, even though the Reference source may be the same for all the questions. These three tests carry 20 marks which forms a part of 100 marks meant for class assignments.

LECTURE METHOD

For certain topics like concept and nature of Reference Service, nature of Reference books, Reference service in different types of libraries, Function of a Reference Department, Qualification of a Reference Librarian, out-put of Reference materials, Psychology of readers. The lectures can be made more lively by quoting interesting case studies drawn from personal experiences of teachers, librarians, as well as students recorded in books dealing with the subject. Some times the lecture method can also be useful to cover the course contents evenly without hindrance to any topics in the syllabus. The success of this method depends upon the students ability to assimilate, understand and grasp the lecture on specific topic.

LIMITATION

The Teaching of Reference Service with the help of above methods developed on the basis of practical experience and wisdom will definitely yield fruitful results. But it is 'difficult' to apply all the above seven methods for teaching Reference Service in conditions obtained in our country today.. The Library Schools or Department of Library Science in our country are suffering from lack of sufficient number of teachers, to spare sufficient time with the students in Reference Department of the Library in which the School/or Department is located and also in some cases lack of proper Reference materials, admitting more number of students, violating the student-teacher ratio prescribed by the U G C Review Committee on Library Science and finally lack of proper coordination and cooperation between the Department of Library Science and the University Library for obtaining the services of experienced Reference Librarians for teaching the subject and trained students in practical reference work on the floor of the reference department.

SUGGESTIONS

The success of teaching of 'Reference Service' in our Indian Library Schools depends upon the following suggestions which need proper implementation :

1. The teacher of ' Reference Service ' should be given sufficient time to work in the Reference Department along with students and also to enable him to prepare himself adequately with the required model questions needed in the method of teaching.
2. As far as possible Reference tools mentioned in the syllabus must be available in the library to which the department is attached, or the departments own library must be strengthened to have all the needed reference sources.
3. The teaching of Reference service should be done within the four walls of Reference Department of a Library rather than in the 'traditional' class room away from the Reference Department so as to have a sort of psychological impact in the minds of the students. This will, facilitate to have instant consultation of any reference work needed in the discussion or lecture method. How far this is possible in our Indian situation ?
4. In the contents of ' Reference Service ' paper, due place must be given to Indian Reference materials. This will enable students to know more about our Indian Reference materials in addition to other important Reference sources from elsewhere.
5. The success of teaching of Library Science in our Indian schools may depend upon the number of students admitted to the course. The admission may be restricted to 20-25 students, so that individual attention can be paid to each student which is all the more necessary for successful teaching of reference service.
6. There should be active cooperation and coordination between the Department of Library Science and the University Library for utilising the resources and services of the Library Staff" and for giving the students more practical training in Reference work.

7. Seminars, symposia or workshops on the methods of teaching and evaluation in Library Science should be conducted at least once in two years for teachers in Library Science to enable them to exchange ideas and opinions with their other colleagues in the profession and formulation of new teaching techniques for improving the quality of teaching in Library Science. The U G C must extend financial support or sponsor such workshops of seminars.

APPENDIX-1

WORKSHEET FOR STUDY AND EVALUATION OF REFERENCE WORKS

1 Name of the student

2 Class

3 Roll No

4 Date

(a) General Guidelines

1 Examine the title page of the document and get the information for the following check points :

  11 Scope of the works

  12 Author's name

  13 Author's degrees; positions, achievements, titles of earlier works.

  14 Publisher—reputation.

  15 Date of publication—Is the work new or based on previous publication

2 Read Preface, Introduction or Foreword for :

  21 Additional information on the scope of the work

  22 Special features claimed

  23 Limitations, if any

  24 Compare with other works on the same subject and with similar scope

3 Examine the work for :

  31 Arrangement—Classified, chronologic, geographic, tabular, or alphabetic

  32 Cross references

  33 Supplementary lists

  34 Indexes

4 Format

41 Physical makeup—binding, paper, type, layout

42 Illustrations—Are the illustrations (colour—black and white) of good quality Are they directly related to the text.

5 Special features ;

51 Distinction—what features distinguish this reference work from all others ?

(b) Guidelines for Study and Evaluation of Encyclopaedias

Note : In studying an Encyclopaedia, the student should follow general guidelines for examining reference works and should also note the following points :

1 Authority :

11 Editor

12 Contributors

13 Publisher

14 Accuracy and up-to-dateness

2 Scope :

21 Purpose

22 Arrangement

23 Adequacy

3 Arrangement :

31 Alphabetical

32 Classified

33 Any other

4 Format and Physical Make-up :

41 General appearance

42 Illustrations

43 Binding

5 Special Features :

51 Supplementary lists or Appendices

52 Errata lists

53 Cross References

6 Method of Keeping Up-to-date :

61 Supplements

62 Annuals

Note : *Appendix I* includes : (a) General guidelines for evaluation and study of reference works; and (b) guidelines for evaluation and study of Encyclopaedias. The above guidelines were prepared, with certain modifications, on the basis of check points listed in Winchell's *Guide to reference books* (7th Edn) and Shoress', *Basic reference sources.* For other types of Reference works, the same method is being followed.

APPENDIX—2

MODEL FIND-ME-OUT QUESTIONS

Note : Mention sources from which you can find out information for the following find-me-out questions.

1 Trace the development of the work 'labour' and its usage.

2 Give Hindi meaning for the word 'Bi-oxalate.'

3 Furnish brief historical information on ' Imperial Sculpture in Roman Art.

4 Furnish brief information on the development and discovery of Business Cycles.

5 Furnish brief information on properties of ' Heavy Water '.

6 Furnish figures pertaining to annual wheat production in Canada for the year 1970.

7 Furnish brief information on Organization of American States.

8 Furnish brief information on UN's activities for the year 1964 relating to 'Permanent Sovereignty over natural resources.'

9 Furnish chronicle of important world evens of January 1953.

10 Furnish the list of resolutions passed by Indian National Congress at its working committee meeting held at Bombay from 12th to 15th March, 1946.

11 Furnish a list of teaching staff members in the Department of Library Science, University of Delhi.

12 Furnish a table pertaining to tidal predictions at London Bridge for June 1971.

13 Furnish a list of Book Clubs in U K.

14 Furnish biographical sketch of Jean delta Fountain.

15 Furnish biographical sketch of S R Ranganathan.

16 Furnish biographical sketch of Sumitranandan Pant.

17 Furnish brief information on Victoria Falls.

18 Furnish brief information on Sarawak.

19 Furnish brief information on Nizampatnam.

20 Furnish brief information about hotels in Hyderabad City.

21 Furnish a list of 'Must-See' places in Paris.

22 Locate a chart pertaining to major world shipping and air routes.

23 Furnish a list of principal mountains in Asia.

24 Who is the Editor of 'Abstracts of World Aledicine'.

25 List the newspapers that are being published from Kent.

26 List out the dailies published from Andhra Pradesh.

27 Name the libraries in South Asia which may have the holdings of the periodicals *Indian farming.*

28 Name the libraries in the United Kingdom which may have the holdings of the periodical *Glasgow courier.*

29 List the essays that were published in English on CENTO during 1965-69.

30 List the articles that were published on 'Education for Librarianship ' during 1967.

31 List the articles that were published in English on 'Hinduism' during April 1964- March 1965.

32 Furnish brief information on non-aligned countries consultative meeting held at Belgrade in July 1969.

33 Furnish brief information on Tamilnadu's river waters accord with Kerala in May 1970.

34 Furnish brief information on Scientific Collaboration agreement between U A R and India in September 1964.

35 Find out who invented the first fountain pen in U S A.

36 Furnish figures as to number of books published on Pure Sciences in U S A in 1967.

37 Furnish figures as to total number of registered medical practitioners in A P in 1958.

38 Furnish figures as to number of scientists and engineers available in India in 1968.

39 Furnish brief information on Oriental foods.

40 Furnish brief information on In-law problems after marriage.

APPENDIX—3
MODEL WORKSHEET FOR ANSWERING FIND-ME-OUT QUESTIONS

1 Name of the student

2 Class

3 Roll No

4 Date

5 Reference Question

6 Exact route followed in locating the Reference tool and for finding the answer ....

....

7 Reference tool in which the answer is located with the following bibliographical details :

 71 Call No

 72 Title

 73 Edition

 74 Collaborator

 75 Year of publication

 76 Imprint

 77 Page numbers which contain the answer

8 No. of reference tools (if it is more than one) consulted in order of preference which you may feel relevant to the answer with bibliographical details as per item No. 7

 91 Total time taken for answering the question

 92 Student's reaction

BIBLIOGRAPHY

1 Bange C A : Library Education and Reference Performance, a Preliminary Report of a Study *(Library journal,* V 92, April 15, 1967, P 1578-8).

2 Benge R C and Dudley E P : Study of Reference Material as Part of Library Education *(Library Association record,* V 58,

November 1956, P 420-424).

3 Ranganathan S R : Evolution of Reference and Documentation Service *(Library Science with slant to documentation,* V 2, N 3, 1965, P 275).

4 Ranganathan S R : Teaching in Library Science (3)—Apprenticeship *(Annals of library science,* V 1, 1954, P 109).

5 Ranganathan S R : Teaching in Library Science (4)—Normative Principles *(Annals of library science,* V 1, 1954, P 162).

6 Ranganathan S R : Training in Library Science (5)—Lecture vs Tutorial Method *(Annals of library science,* V 1, 1954, P 252).

7 Ranganathan S R : Training for Librarianship *(Annals of library science,* V 5, N 2, 1958, P 55).

8 Gangadhara Rao P : Reference Work, Reference Service, Definition *(Library science with slant to Documentation,* V 3, N 1, 1966, P 51).

9 Abdul Rahman : Philosophy of Reference Service *(Annals of library science,* V 8, N 4, December 1961, P 150),

10 Abdul Rahman : Teaching Reference Service *(Library science with slant to documentation,* V 3, N 4, December 1966, P 343-361).

11 Benge R C : *Study of reference material.* Rev Edn 2. Purely (Survey), London & Home Counties Branch of the Library Association. 1962.

Index